WOMEN
of COLOR
PRAY

WOMEN

of COLOR

PRAY

Voices of Strength, Faith, Healing, Hope and Courage

Edited and with introductions by

CHRISTAL M. JACKSON

Walking Together, Finding the Way
SKYLIGHT PATHS Publishing
Woodstock, Vermont

Women of Color Pray:
Voices of Strength, Faith, Healing, Hope and Courage

2005 First Printing
© 2005 by Christal M. Jackson

Page 159 constitutes a continuation of this copyright page.

Library of Congress Cataloging-in-Publication Data
Women of color pray : voices of strength, faith, healing, hope, and courage / edited and with introductions by Christal M. Jackson.
    p. cm.
Includes index.
ISBN 1-59473-077-6 (pbk.)
1. Women, Black—Religious life. 2. African American women—Religious life. 3. Women—Religious life. I. Jackson, Christal M.
BL625.7.W635 2005
204'.3'082—dc22   2005006157

10   9   8   7   6   5   4   3   2   1

Manufactured in the United States of America
Cover Design: Jenny Buono
Kente cloth design on cover courtesy of www.storyclothfabrics.com

SkyLight Paths Publishing is creating a place where people of different spiritual traditions come together for challenge and inspiration, a place where we can help each other understand the mystery that lies at the heart of our existence.

SkyLight Paths sees both believers and seekers as a community that increasingly transcends traditional boundaries of religion and denomination—people wanting to learn from each other, *walking together, finding the way.*

SkyLight Paths, "Walking Together, Finding the Way," and colophon are trademarks of LongHill Partners, Inc., registered in the U.S. Patent and Trademark Office.

Walking Together, Finding the Way
Published by SkyLight Paths Publishing
A Division of LongHill Partners, Inc.
Sunset Farm Offices, Route 4, P.O. Box 237
Woodstock, VT 05091
Tel: (802) 457-4000   Fax: (802) 457-4004
www.skylightpaths.com

In memory of my aunt
Lee "Sister" Potts
May 11, 1943–February 26, 2003
I truly miss you, but I'm grateful for every memory

In memory of my great aunts
Corrine "Aunt Teen" Virginia Eggleston Marshall
October 15, 1909–March 22, 2003
and
Priscilla Stewart
December 22, 1914–December 22, 1993
That which you instilled in my mother has blessed me

In honor of my mother
Bobbie W. Jackson
Your prayers have covered and guided me through dangers seen and unseen, and I'm eternally grateful

With love for my aunts
Helena Jones, Eddie Mae Jackson, and Gladys Neal

With hope for my beloved nieces and nephew
Essence, Jalisa, and Joshua Jackson
I pray that you will grow to live lives that glorify God

Contents

Introduction

When I was four years old, my mother taught me the Lord's Prayer. At that age I could not articulate the way I felt, but I knew that praying was a different experience, an important element in my development. It was sweet as she knelt beside me. As we clasped our hands, I knew that this was serious. Little did I know then that this bedtime ritual would be the force that defines my life and impacts those around me as well. Women of color pray and have prayed out of necessity for survival, out of love for the Divine, and because we believe in the power of prayer. Prayer has been the prevailing force behind the education of our children, protection and courage for our men, hope for our daughters, and the balm that heals sorrows. Many times I have been taken hostage by prayer and forced into submission to pray for others and even to cry out on my own behalf. Prayer is invisible, yet it's so invincible.

Historically, women of color from all around the world share one very similar and distinct characteristic—we possess an unusual sense of spirituality. No matter what our faith tradition, we are fully cognizant of the fact that there is something greater than ourselves that exists, and this power is the final authority in our lives. This desire for God is fostered by the environment that shapes our world. Our environment is not always positive and affirming, so we are forced to create a hallowed space for ourselves and our loved ones.

It is the impact of our environment that often determines where and how we express our love of God. Societal and cultural implications are often the gatekeepers of our faith. The collection of pieces in this book reflect this reality. Women of color from different faiths and experiences express through words their perception of God in defining who we are as women.

As I put this book together, I was intrigued by the collective diversity of women of color. Although the pieces chronologically cover many generations, each woman's words are relevant for today. Harriet Tubman and Phillis Wheatley represent an era in American history when women of color were suffering under the hand of slavery. Their work is powerful because they speak of God in a way that, even in the midst of suffering, forces us to renew our faith and believe in the impossible. It challenges women of all walks of life not to settle for second best. Contemporary poet Akasha Gloria Hull gives voice to spiritual power as a form of resistance. As we resist the presence of evil in the world, we make room for God. This sentiment is echoed throughout the works of Native American and Asian women as well. Native American women pray out of a situation of displacement that is different from that of African American women. African Americans are displaced because their ancestors were brought to this country against their will. Native Americans are in their home country, but have been displaced to reservations. They have great reverence for the natural elements of the earth, which they feel connects them even more to God. Linda Hogan and Geraldine Kudaka give voice to the strength of their mothers. Our mothers are the teachers and keepers of the faith. Sandra Cisneros gives voice to the power of culture through which we show our love for family and our interconnectedness throughout generations. It is nearly impossible for women of color to see ourselves outside of our cultures.

To ask us to choose between faith and culture creates an inner conflict that causes a great deal of turmoil.

These women, like all of the wonderfully gifted women in this collection, are creative and powerful. As you journey through the pages you will also witness the voices of jazz vocalist Rachelle Ferrell and gospel sensations Yolanda Adams and CeCe Winans. Each of them brings a different sense of the power of prayer. Other women, members of a spiritual group who call themselves the Universal Foundation for Better Living, have collaborated to reinterpret the traditional Christian Lord's Prayer from various perspectives of women and children of color, and you'll find those prayers appearing in several sections of this book.

In a post-9/11 society, prayer has been validated. Women of color all around the globe are praying that terror, which has been a unique part of their past, will not destroy the future of our world. Prayer changes people and situations.

PRAYER IN CREATION

God is the source of all creation. With God as the source of all creation, prayer is the midwife. This partnership has existed since the creation of humankind. This relationship is mirrored in the lives of women of color in numerous ways. Throughout history we have managed to give birth to nations of people in the midst of difficult times. These nations of people have been able to give birth to dreams and build a future for themselves and their descendents. Their descendents have continued to live out their legacy and continue to build.

Women of color in the Bible offer a glimpse into the power of this relationship. Hannah prayed for a son, Hagar prayed as she faced the dilemma of birthing a son, and Leah prayed and she conceived a son. Prayer was used whenever women needed to confront the reality of their lives and create a new world for themselves and their people. Creation is not limited to the birth of a child but extends to the birth of dreams and visions. This relationship with the Divine is still strong hundreds of generations later. And the characteristics of this relationship are shaped by cultural differences. Depending on what part of the world we are from, the prayer ritual may look different, but the essence of the ritual is the same.

What have women of color created through prayer? Churches, strong families, resilient children, courageous husbands, a nation conscious of the need for racial healing, congressmen and congresswomen, engineers, educators, astronauts, designers, hope, joy, integrity, and peace of mind. The prayers of women of color will live beyond our years. Our prayers will change the world. Our prayers will give God a physical presence in the world through our offspring. Our prayers will lead to the discovery of cures for diseases. Our prayers will end injustice. Our prayers will correct ill thoughts and ungodly actions. The world needs us to continue praying.

PRAYER AS RESISTANCE

"Life for me ain't been no crystal stair" is a line from "Mother to Son," by the famous African American poet Langston Hughes, yet it is an experience not limited to African American women. Women of color know all too well the struggle for equality and the pain of racism. Even in the face of unimaginable anguish, our ability to pray could not be daunted. We prayed in cotton fields, on tobacco plantations, as our children were being sold, as our men were being dehumanized, as our culture was being annihilated, as we toiled in slavery, and even while being raped. We knew that if we could manage to tell God our struggles, then our present reality would not be the inevitable plight of our sons and daughters. Latina women know well the battles they face against poverty and the dangers and degradation of escaping their homelands in search of a better life—only to find that the system they seek to be a part of is not always sensitive to their culture. Native Americans and Asian immigrants know the horror of being uprooted and estranged from their homelands.

Prayer as resistance is indeed a characteristic of God, for it is a clear demonstration of God's power over evil. What a powerful testament to the faith and courage of women of color to know that we would seek God in our time of need. It is one thing to know God in times of joy, but to believe that God exists in the midst of despair and suffering is different. A distress cry is a call of faith.

Women who pray through adversity are resisting societal evils and negative social pressure. This is the prayer of true resistance. When women of color can still find their way to God in a cold world, we have demonstrated the prayer of resistance. The prayer of resistance is steadfast.

PRAYER AS THE LANGUAGE OF LOVE

Love is a universal language that the blind can see, the mute can speak, and the deaf can hear. It transcends logic and defies the rules of science. Love cannot be denied. Women of color simply love God. This love is not rational, but it is built on an incomprehensible trust birthed out of experience.

Every time God changes the lives of women of color, this bond is strengthened. Prayer enhances the relationship, and we continue to seek God, serve God, and love God. The beauty of God's nature is that God desires to commune with that which God has created. Prayer secures this bond.

God's love is manifested in our personal relationships, and it becomes the defining force behind our actions. It is always amazing to witness faith in action in the lives of women of color. We will pray to God and then demonstrate our faith in God with an intensity that cannot be shaken, because of our love for God.

Some of the pieces in this book reflect the intensity of this love relationship as a visual image—a woman lost in love, a dreamy kind of love that leaves her speechless and even motionless. Totally consumed in the moment, swept away in wonder, mesmerized by God's provision, humbled by God's steadfast mercy, encouraged by God's random acts of grace, smitten by God's power—this characterizes the love between God and women of color.

This love perfects our faith because we can live life with the expectation that the one we love will be there for us. We live with an assurance that the experiences of life will not consume us because of God's presence.

Women of color know that God's love is real, and it is realized through every definitive act of God's love.

OUT OF AFRICA

In preparing this book and reading the pieces, I was amazed to find that at times all of the women sounded as if they were speaking or crying from the same place. Women of color are not monolithic, nor are our principles of faith, but our struggles and triumphs bear many of the same marks. This may be due in part to the history of humanity. Scientists contend that the earliest ancestors of Homo sapiens lived in Africa. From these prehistoric mothers came many nations and groups of people that covered and populated the earth. Our prayers bear witness to this experience.

Women of Africa have long been known for their spiritual prowess. Prayer is birthed out of their understanding of who God is. All of life is considered sacred and cyclical. Therefore, their focus is not on the afterlife but rather on living life to the fullest in the present, so that as life is recycled blessings will follow. It is believed that the ancestors are no longer present in the natural world but become spirits that direct life on earth.

The prayer life of women of Africa reflects their strong belief that everything develops in the cosmos. Be it good or bad, all of life is controlled by the spirit world. Women of earlier times were familiar with gods and deities that they could use to channel spiritual power. Unlike in traditional Western societies, women played an integral role in shaping the spiritual lives of their communities. However, there is not much information recorded, since African societies relied heavily on transmitting culture through the spoken word.

MIGRATION

As women moved outward from Africa to other parts of the world, their religious beliefs were modified to reflect the new cultures of which they became a part. Their fundamental understanding of the nature of good and evil made the transitions easier. African slaves quickly assimilated Christianity, although traditional African religions ascribe to the belief that there are numerous gods. Interestingly enough, these religions connect to these gods by summoning their presence through various rituals, just as Christians seek the Holy Spirit to connect with God. Culture plays a major role in prayer, in that it places definition around who God is and the actions of God.

The prayers of Asian women reflect a belief in good and evil as well. Their prayers speak to the importance of intimacy with God and of tranquility. This intimacy and tranquility can only be achieved by nurturing the relationship with the Divine, which directly impacts all areas of life. Everything is interconnected, and once there has been a disruption in the spirit world, the individual has to work to reunite with the Divine. This is reflected in the profound discipline in Asian traditions such as Buddhism, Confucianism, and Hinduism. Much like traditional African religions, Asian religions rely heavily on deities to channel the spirit world to the natural world.

The women of the Middle East offer prayers that are quite relational. In their communication with God, they give the impression that this God force is their close companion. It is as if they possess the power of God, and therefore their actions are a direct reflection of God's nature.

Women of African descent in modern America are still viewed as the spiritual nucleus of their families and communities. This is reflected in the pieces that speak of the pain and struggle of our experience as well as our hopes for our children. Prayers of women of color are generally communal in nature—rarely will you find us praying for ourselves, but we're always lifting up those around us. The only time that our prayers seem individualistic is when they are introspective in nature and we are seeking a deeper relationship or level of communion. This, in turn, is intended to make us better for service.

Reality changed for women of color who migrated to other parts of the world, and prayer life reflected the changes in their status and culture. We were often forced to change, so our prayer language reflects resistance against oppressive systems and hope for the future. Our prayers also reflect our attempts to hold onto our culture while integrating ourselves into our newfound society. Our prayers turn into poetry and lyrics of songs, which possess the power to move the hearts and minds of people.

Our prayers speak to our determination never to give up, our fight for self-definition and freedom, and our love of God. Collectively as women we have struggled and continue to struggle to define our place in this world, but without question we are a spiritual force in the lives of those we touch. God gives us a sense of purpose and belonging. Spirituality is for women of color what air is to human life. We are sustained by God's presence. In the face of social frustration, we are certain that God's power will prevail. In the face of familial and relational strife, our hope is rooted in the full knowledge that God is for us.

THE JOURNEY

In the Christian tradition there is a hymn that says, "We've come this far by faith," and yes, women of color have come a long way—and we are still in the process of becoming. That is truly the beauty of being in relationship with God. The more we communicate with God through prayer, the more of God we experience. As women of color, this journey to relationship with God presents many challenges and triumphs. In today's society, prayer is not as elusive as it once was, nor is it confined to traditional settings. Poets and songwriters have taken their places in pronouncing their belief in God through music and writing, bearing witness to the fact that women of color are experiencing the spiritual freedom necessary for the world to see God through our eyes. Unlike in earlier days when women were not allowed to speak publicly of God without ridicule, or when they feared to speak of the God of their experience, society has evolved. It is because of our continuous prayer and spiritual fervor that the world has come to acknowledge the value of our prayers. That this book is a collection of prayers by women of color throughout the ages and from different traditions illustrates that our voices have been and are powerful and influential.

Though the vast majority of the prayers in this book were written by women of color, there are a few exceptions. The Twenty-third Psalm is included because it is one of the biblical passages that are hallmarks of the African American church. It was the first passage of scripture that I was required to memorize in its entirety. The elders taught me that it is the psalm to recite when facing fear, and for years it has been my solace in times of trouble. I can vividly recall times in my childhood when I recited this scripture in the face of danger and it brought me peace. I have included a few traditional hymns and spirituals for the same reason—though they may not have been written by a woman of color, they have long been sung or recited as our prayers and are sources of comfort and strength for us today.

I have also included a few Buddhist affirmations that were probably not written by women. But reading them immediately made me think of my Asian sisters and their need to feel protected. I feel that these affirmations offer the same feelings of peace and protection that I have drawn from the Twenty-third Psalm and traditional songs.

Now that our spiritual voices are recognized and applauded, the question then becomes, Where do we go from here? The answer is quite simple: Forward. Move forward as the voice of liberation for the pain and suffering of all people. Forward as the hope of the nation for those who have lost hope in God. Forward as the conqueror of evil in any form. Forward as the woman that God recognizes and seeks communion with. Women of color must continue the journey of prayer.

Like its predecessor *Women Pray: Voices through the Ages, from Many Faiths, Cultures, and Traditions*, edited by Monica Furlong, *Women of Color Pray* is divided into sections. The first section looks at faith, the medium through which women of color connect with God. This is a clear demonstration of our awareness that God does exist and, more important, that God is necessary for our existence. Prayer is built on that principle. It is impossible to pray without having an assurance that your prayer is being heard. Women of color place our faith in the power of God because we are aware of what God has done for us in the past and mindful of God's ability in the future. Our faith is pronounced in the selected pieces. Our faith in God gives us the ability to have faith in ourselves and in others, which unmistakably impacts the world at large. The beauty of faith is that we share it with our community, and our community is empowered by our faith. This is what keeps the legacy of prayer alive—faith in action.

The next section shows our strength. In the face of insurmountable trials filled with emotional horrors and physical distress, women of color manage to overcome obstacles set before us and gain wisdom for generations to come. Our experiences do not destroy us but instead build our character. Women of color are strong. The writings come from voices of strength. Where does the strength come from? God. Recognizing our source, we incessantly seek God in prayer. Oftentimes strength is spoken of in the limited terms of physical capability. However, it is important to know that strength can be measured by an individual's response to a bad situation. Women of color are not easily swayed by circumstances; we seek the path of God in whatever direction life takes us.

The third section focuses on hope. We are able to continue regardless of circumstances because we are keenly aware that our tomorrow will be better than our today. We know that we want more for our children than we experienced. The greatest gift that anyone could give is the gift of hope. Prayer gives hope. It renders an unusual type of hope. Women of color hoped for a world that we are beginning to see. As for those who didn't live to see their hope realized in the natural world, they are bearing witness as immortal beings to the gift of hope.

The theme of the next section is healing. With a sure awareness that our lives are connected to the source of life, we are the conduit of the power of God. True healing can only take place through the power of God. Women of color are the perfect conduits of healing because we know all too well the pain of being broken. In these selections you will hear our anguish over life's trials and disappointments, but you will also feel the balm of our words, the realization that some of life's scars are so indelible that only God has the power to heal them. This is one of the reasons that prayer is such a delight, because we are returning to the source of our creation for a touch.

The final section speaks of courage. Women of color are often afraid, but we are still determined to move forward. To be afraid to remain in our current situation and yet be apprehensive about change is part of the formula for courage. Another part is knowing that a decision must be made despite the outcome. Courage is the act of confronting your deepest fears, and women of color constantly confront our fears through prayer. Our issues and circumstances often seem to be much larger than we are, but our voices lifted in prayer topple any mountain set before us. This strength comes from prayer against our situation and prayer even for those who seek to destroy us. What manner of courage it takes to place your life in the hands of God, even in the midst of obvious danger and rejection. Women of color are courageous because we feel the force of God on our side.

Women of color pray that the eternal presence of God will be real in the lives of people. Prayer is the most wonderful gift that I've been granted. The selections that follow are gifts that will illuminate your journey, cause you to smile, speak to your situation, and, more important, echo the words of a diverse and beautiful group of women.

1

FAITH

Faith is an invisible force that seeks to make visible the reality of God at work in the world through people. It is impossible to carry out the will of God without the presence of faith. Faith is a discipline, a lifestyle, a witness, a reality in perpetual pursuit of communion with God. Women of color have faith that can be witnessed in prayer language. Felt in our compassion. Embraced in our work and creative ability.

This group of pieces makes evident the persistence of our faith. For an enslaved woman, faith in God is the key to freedom. For a daughter estranged from her land, faith is the principle that guides her home. Whatever the circumstance surrounding our physical reality, it cannot direct the course of our faith. Faith forces its way through a sea of impossibility when no clear way is in sight. Our faith is not fueled by what we can see but rather by what our spirit beholds. Our spirit is awakened by the presence of God's spirit, which illuminates our journey. Women of color understand that life is a journey, always arriving at new locations and experiences but never settled by the comfort of familiarity. We are motivated to journey forward because our ancestors are cheering for us, and our family and community are depending on us to believe the impossible.

Gilbert then thought of the words of his mother, whispered to him from the auction block:

> Trust in the Lord,
> And you'll overcome,
> Somehow,
> Somewhere,
> Someday!

"Oh Lord," inquired Isabella, "what is this slavery, that it can do such dreadful things? What evil can it not do?" Well may she ask; for surely the evils it can and does do, daily and hourly, can never be summed up, till we can see them as they are recorded by him who writes no errors, and reckons without mistake. This account, which now varies so widely in the estimate of different minds, will be viewed alike by all.

Harriet Tubman

I do something every day.
Something.
Whether it's light a candle, or still myself, or
reconstruct myself, or say my affirmations, or
    thank the universe.
But something every day.
I think that if I don't, I won't live.
And I won't be powerful if I don't, because I also
    know that that's what's historically kept us
    alive, that touch with other worlds and other
    experiences.
Or we wouldn't have had stories about people
    walking on the water back to Africa.
So I cannot exist and not pay homage to that.
I can't.
Otherwise I would stop existing just like that
    (snaps her fingers).
So that's why I have to do something every day.
It's like the first breath is that acknowledgement.
I used to be into yoga a lot and tai chi, but right
    now I'm not.

Now it seems to me more about breath and
    prayer and joining the universe every twenty-
    four hours.

Masani Alexis De Veaux

Lord, I want to be free of the pressure to do great things in the world by being great in doing small things for Thee.

Marian Wright Edelman

One day soon, Native peoples and our religions, national identities, and sovereignty can emerge from the shadows into which we have been cast by the immigrants. In the full light of day—the light we cast on ourselves, that is—we can live long and prosper.

Paula Gunn Allen

A SLAVE WOMAN'S PRAYER

O Lord, bless my master. When he calls upon thee to damn his soul, do not hear him, do not hear him, but hear me—save him—make him know he is wicked, and he will pray to thee.

I am afraid, O Lord, I have wished him bad wishes in my heart—keep me from wishing him bad—though he whips me and beats me sore, tell me of my sins, and make me pray more to thee—make me more glad for what thou hast done for me, a poor Negro.

Anonymous slave woman

A PREGNANT MOTHER'S PRAYER

God, I thank You for and ask Your blessing
On this child growing within me.
Keep her or him and me healthy and strong to
Begin our lives together safe and sound.

Marian Wright Edelman

PRAYER FOR DISCOVERY

Father, I thank you that before we ever begin our search for you, you have already found us, I am so glad to be found of you! Help others in their search and discovery.
Amen.

Marjorie L. Kimbrough

Potential of my soul, in your nature is wholeness.
Your fulfillment is done in the world of
    manifestation, as it is in the spiritual realm.
Give us our daily substance, from which all
    things come.
We are released from the belief in limitations as
    we release others, by seeing the unlimited
    potential in ourselves and others.
Do not let us lapse into duality; instead let us so
    use the principle that we do not slip into that
    state of believing there is an evil one.
Take us to a place where we know there is only
    One. Amen.

Rev. Dr. Sheila McKeithen, Rev. Dr. Anna Price,
and Rev. Dr. Mary Tumpkin

ATONEMENT

When I write,
I am at one with God.
I sit in stillness,
Pen in hand,
Fresh page open
To receive
The Word.
Enveloped in sacred silence,
Radiant with anticipation,
I wait.
My mind soars,
My spirit quickens,
My body resonates,
And then,
The Idea.
Sometimes it unfolds slowly,
Gaining momentum as I massage it into words.
Other times it strikes with a force
That takes my breath away,
And I write vigorously to keep up.

My emotions swell and oscillate
From awe,
To pain,
To love,
To joy,
To gratitude,
And ultimately,
Back to awe,
As, in a moment of illumination,
I remember
Who I Am.

Tawnicia Ferguson Rowan

OTHERS MAY FORGET YOU

Others may forget you, but not I.
I am haunted by your beautiful ghost.

Empress Yamatohime

OBLATION

At your feet, God, we bow because you are
  worthy
The fruit of our lips and the labor of our hands
  we give to thee
As sun-kissed daughters of Zion we leap from the
  throne of grace
into a world submerged with your Grace. Amen.

Christal M. Jackson

O Mother, my heart is being torn by this pain of
    separation!
Why does Your heart not melt seeing this endless
    stream of tears?
O Mother, many Great Souls have adored You
and thereby attained Your Vision and become
    eternally one with You.
O Darling Mother! Please open the doors of
    Your compassionate heart to this humble
    servant of Yours!
I am suffocating like one who is drowning.
If you are not willing to come to me,
then please put an end to my life.
Let the sword with which You behead the cruel
    and unrighteous
fall on my head as well.
At least, let me be blessed by the touch of Your
    sword!
What sense is there in keeping this useless body
    which is a heavy burden for me?

Savitri L. Bess

ON BEING BROUGHT FROM AFRICA TO AMERICA

'Twas mercy brought me from my Pagan land,
Taught my heightened soul to understand
That there's a God, that there's a Saviour too;
Once I redemption neither sought nor knew.
Some view our race with scornful eye,
"Their color is a diabolic dye."
Remember, Christians, Negroes, black as Cain,
May be refined, and join th' angelic train.

Phillis Wheatley

SIX BROTHERS

In Grimms' fairytale "The Six Swans," a sister keeps a six-year silence and weaves six thistle shirts to break the spell that has changed her brothers into swans. She weaves all but the left sleeve of the final shirt, and when the brothers are changed back into men, the youngest lacks only his left arm and has in its place a swan's wing.

In Spanish our name means swan.
A great past—castles maybe
or a Sahara city,
but more likely
a name that stuck
to a barefoot boy
herding the dusty flock
down the bright road.

We'll never know.
Great-grandparents might
but family likes to keep to silence—
perhaps with reason
though we don't need far back to go.

On our father's side we have a cousin,
second, but cousin nonetheless,
who shot someone, his wife I think.
And on the other hand, there's
mother's brother who shot himself.

Then there's us —
seven ways to make the name or break it.
Our father has it planned:
oldest, you're doctor,
second, administration,
me, he shrugs, you should've been reporting
    weather,
next, musician,
athlete,
genius,
and youngest — well,
you'll take the business over.

You six a team
keeping to the master plan,
the lovely motion of tradition.
Appearances are everything.
We live for each other's expectations.
Brothers, it is so hard to keep up with you.

I've got the bad blood in me I think,
the mad uncle, the bite of the bullet.

Ask me anything.
Six thistle shirts. Keep a vow of silence.
I'll do it. But I'm earthbound
always in my admiration.
My six brothers, graceful, strong.
Except for you, the little one-winged,
finding it as difficult as me
to keep the good name clean.

Sandra Cisneros

BLESSINGS

If a child is beautiful but has no character,
He is no more than a wooden doll.
Good character is the beauty of a person.
A woman can be as beautiful as Egbara [a
    beautiful rat]
If she has no character,
She is no more than a wooden doll.
A man may be very very handsome,
Like a fish in the water.
If he has no good character,
He is no more than a wooden doll.

Yoruba priestess

THOUGHTS ON THE WORKS OF PROVIDENCE

But see the sons of vegetation rise,
And spread their leafy banners to the skies.
All-wise Almighty providence we trace
In trees, and plants, and all the flow'ry race;
As clear as in the nobler frame of man,
All lovely copies of the Maker's plan.
The pow'r the same that forms a ray of light
That call'd creation from eternal night.
"Let there be light," he said: from his profound
Old chaos heard, and trembled at the sound:
Swift as word, inspir'd by pow'r divine,
Behold the light around its maker shine,
The first fair product of th' omnific God,
And now through all his works diffus'd abroad.

Phillis Wheatley

IN WHARTON, TEXAS

for my grandpa

Good Lawd, thank you for letting me see
    another day.
Thank you that my lying down was not the end.
Thank you for the food on my table, shoes on my
    feet, and the activity of my limbs.
Bless my family and my enemies too.
Lawd, we just wanna do your will.

Christal M. Jackson

SLAVE NARRATIVES

My children, there is a God, who hears and sees you." "A God, mau-mau! Where does he live?" asked the children. "He lives in the sky," she replied; "and when you are beaten, or cruelly treated, or fall into any trouble, you must ask help of him, and he will always hear and help you."

Sojourner Truth

A SLAVE MOTHER'S DOLEFUL PRAYER

We stopped at this boarding house. This was our first night's stop after leaving Wilmington [Delaware]. The keeper of the boarding house tried to buy Fannie Woods' baby, but there was a disagreement regarding the price. About five next morning we started on. When we had gone about half a mile a colored boy came running down the road with a message from his master, and we were halted until his master came bringing a colored woman with him, and he bought the baby out of Fannie Woods' arms.

As the colored woman was ordered to take it away I heard Fannie Woods' cry, "O God, I would rather hear the clods fall on the coffin lid of my child than to hear its cries because it is taken away from me." She said, "good bye, child." We were ordered to move on, and could hear the crying of the child in the distance as it was borne away by the other woman, and I could hear the deep sobs of a broken hearted mother. We could hear the groans of many as they prayed for God to have mercy upon us, and give us grace to endure the hard trials though which we must pass.

Slave narrative

STARS ARE SHINING

O my Lord, stars are shining
And the eyes of men are closed.
Kings have shut their doors
And every lover is alone with his beloved.
Here I am alone with you.

Rabi'a Al-Adawiyya

STEAL AWAY TO JESUS

Steal away,
Steal away,
Steal away to Jesus!

Steal away,
Steal away home,
I ain't got long to stay here.

Steal away,
Steal away,
Steal away to Jesus!

Steal away,
Steal away home,
I ain't got long to stay here.

My Lord, He calls me,
He calls me by the thunder,
The trumpet sounds within my soul,
I ain't got long to stay here.

Negro spiritual

WOMEN'S MORNING SONG

Morning has risen;
O, Asobe, take away from our path
Every hurt,
Every pain,
Every sickness,
All our cares.
O, Asobe, bring us home safely tonight.

Pygmy women

TROUBLIN' THE WATER

Wade in the water,
Wade in the water, children,
Wade in the water,
God's gonna trouble the water.

Negro spiritual

JUST A CLOSER WALK WITH THEE

Just a closer walk with Thee;
Grant it, Jesus, if you please,
Daily walking close with Thee,
Let it be, dear Lord, let it be.
I am weak but Thou art strong,
Jesus, keep me from all wrong,
I'll be satisfied as long,
As I walk, let me walk close with Thee.
Through this world of toils and snares,
If I falter, Lord, who cares?
Who with me my burden shares?
None but Thee, dear Lord, none but Thee.
When my feeble life is o'er,
Time for me won't be no more,
Guide me gently, safely o'er,
To Thy kingdom shore, to Thy shore.

Traditional hymn

2

STRENGTH

Life requires women of color to be strong. We are responsible not only for ourselves but also for our family and community. It is because of our enduring strength that generations have survived, thrived, and resisted when necessary to claim their space.

The spiritual strength of women of color is the pillar of our community. Our experiences don't destroy us but rather build our character, enabling us to pass our wisdom on to the next generations. Our stories of struggle give way to the beauty of our triumphs. Women of color don't buckle under adversity but pray through the circumstances. God's response affirms our strength. Our strength is a birthmark from God that makes us beautiful and unique. Although we are strong, we are gentle. Women of color are as fragile as glass while being made of steel. This duality makes us a mystery to humankind and at times even to ourselves, but beloved by God. These pieces reflect the duality of our strength. We are strong enough to be gentle and gentle enough to undergird our community.

I THE WOMAN

I
am she
of your stories
the notorious
one
leg wrapped
around
the door
bare heart
sticking
like a burr
the fault
the back street
the weakness
that's me

I'm the Thursday
night
the poor
excuse

I'm she
I'm dark
in the veins
I'm
intoxicant
I'm hip
and good skin
brass
and sharp tooth
hard lip pushed
against
the air
I'm lightbeam
no stopping me

I am
your temporary
thing
your own
mad
dancing
I am
a live wildness
left
behind
one earring

in the car
a finger-
print
on skin
the black smoke
in your
clothes
and in
your
mouth

Sandra Cisneros

Supreme Presence
That dwells in higher consciousness
Sacred by Nature
The time is now, Your purpose is manifest
In Spirit, Soul and Body
by Directed Inspiration
Use this moment
For life, love, wisdom, substance and power
Forgive us for our own belief
in separation
As we commune with Spirit
Ordain our decisions from error thoughts
Anoint us now

Wendy Gordon, Susan Newbold, Deborah
Sharperson, and Cherlyn Taylor

THE TAO TE CHING

The weakest thing in the world
excels the strongest thing in the world
what doesn't exist finds room where there is none
thus we know doing nothing succeeds

teaching without words
succeeding without effort
few in the world can equal this.

Buddhist affirmation

THE SOUND OF SILENCE

Listen ...
to the contented melodies of a free bird,
to spring raindrops communing with the earth,
to the trees dancing in a summer breeze,
to the flowing stream, hastening to reunite with
    its source,
to the rhythmic cadence of a baby's breath,
to the synchronized footsteps of strolling lovers,
to the burning desires of your heart.
It is the sound of silence.
It is the voice of God.

Tawnicia Ferguson Rowan

The white wind
that encircles her is a part
just as
the blue sky
hanging in turquoise from her neck.

Joy Harjo

We have the power and responsibility to create peace and happiness in our lives and to ease the suffering in our world.

Susan L. Taylor

The Tao never does a thing
yet there is nothing it doesn't do
if a ruler could uphold it
people by themselves would change
and changing if their desires stirred
he could make them still
with simplicity that has no name
stilled by nameless simplicity
they would not desire
and not desiring be at peace
the world would fix itself

Buddhist affirmation

THE LANGUAGE OF ENDANGERMENT

the language of endangerment
means language that endangers
language that defends
means language that stretches boundaries
& opens new doors.

the language of endangerment
are words from people under attack
a world under attack
the earth, trees & sky endangered
by a selfish & money-driven culture …

we are the people who speak the words &
    language
of endangerment
we speak words that endanger lies …
our hearts are open
our spirits are free
we speak
we speak

we listen & learn ...
the language of endangerment pounds in our ears
courses thru our blood
threatens us no more.

Victoria Lena Manyarrows

So often we wallow in our children's problems rather than exult in their strengths and possibilities. So often we dwell on the things that seem impossible rather than on the things that are possible. So often we are depressed by what remains to be done and forget to be thankful for all that has been done.

Forgive us, God.

Marian Wright Edelman

This land is the house
we have always lived in.
The women,
their bones are holding up the earth.

Linda Hogan

For up here where we live, our life is one continuous fight for food and for clothing and a
struggle against bad hunting and snowstorms
and sickness.

That is all I can tell you about the world,
both the one I know and the one I don't know.

Inuit woman

LAMENT OF MARY FOR HER SON

I am overwhelmed, O my son,
I am overwhelmed by love
And I cannot endure
That I should be in the chamber
And you on the wood of a cross
I in the house
And you in the tomb.

Anonymous Syrian woman

BIRTHRIGHT

i am the crazy woman
who killed her mother
i wear nikon lenses
for eyes
and lie thru the skin
of my teeth
nicotine rows aligned by
braces
locks, and window fixtures
i go crazy
stripping
off wallpaper
i paint my nails red
i leave the lover
i loved most,
sent postcards
from the coast, little
notes saying
"on the way to the embassy
i lost my smile …"

i like strange men
whose intimacy
gives them power
i write without alliance
i take on improbability
with the fury
of a hellcat and rub
my silk collar
against my nose
i am the crazy woman
who is not
so crazy after all
i lied when i said
i killed my mother
in my womb, i am carrying her
our birthright fur
blood & spit ...

Geraldine Kudaka

Small wonder that far too many Native people, especially children, are suicidal. It is not that we possess a death wish but that the huge culture around us projects its homicidal wish onto us.

Paula Gunn Allen

BABY SUGGS'S SATURDAY AFTERNOON "SERMON"

Then she shouted, "Let the children come!" and they ran from the trees toward her.

"Let your mothers hear you laugh," she told them, and the woods rang. The adults looked on and could not help smiling.

Then "Let the grown men come," she shouted. They stepped out one by one from among the ringing trees.

"Let your wives and your children see you dance," she told them, and groundlife shuddered under their feet.

Finally she called the women to her. "Cry," she told them. "For the living and the dead. Just cry." And without covering their eyes the women let loose.

… In the silence that followed, Baby Suggs, holy, offered up to them her great big heart.

She did not tell them to clean up their lives or to go and sin no more. She did not tell them they were the blessed of the earth, its inheriting meek or its glorybound pure.

She told them that the only grace they could have was the grace they could imagine. That if they could not see it, they would not have it.

"Here," she said, "in this place, we flesh; flesh that weeps, laughs; flesh that dances on bare feet in grass. Love it. Love it hard. Yonder they do not love your flesh. They despise it. They don't love your eyes; they'd just as soon pick em out. No more do they love the skin on your back. Yonder they flay it. And O my people they do not love your hands. Those they only use, tie, bind, chop off and leave empty. Love your hands! Love them. Raise them up and kiss them. Touch others with them, pat them together, stroke them on your face 'cause they don't love that either. *You* got to love it, *you!*"

Toni Morrison

COVER ME WITH NIGHT

Come Lord,
And cover me with the night.
Spread your grace over us
As you assured us you would.
Your promises are more than
All the stars in the sky;
Your mercy is deeper than the night.
Lord, it will be cold.
The night comes with its breath of death.
Night comes; the end comes; you come.
Lord, we will wait for you
Day and night.

Ashanti women, Ghana

All-inclusive Source of our good, Your nature is
    whole, perfect and complete.

Allow your splendor to pour forth.

I surrender my foolish will to the awareness of
    Your divine plan.

I know that You provide for my every need, at
    every moment, in every way.

I free myself, others, and all thoughts that keep
    me bound, as Your supreme love has set me
    free.

Thank you, that there is only one power and one
    presence, therefore there is no evil.

All the praise, power, wisdom, and authority are
    Yours forever. Amen.

Norma Eaton, Dr. Phyllis Green, Marcia Grubb,
and Jacqui Vanterpool

3

HOPE

Hope represents the birthplace of creation. In order to meet the demands of life and in the face of the impossible, women of color summon and surrender to the power of hope. This power overcomes the pain of our environment and allows birthing to begin. Hope is important for us to continue our fight to define who we are as women and to give life to those around us. Women of color pray simply because we hope that God will hear us and respond.

This birthing is labor-intensive and guided by a passion and fire that can't be quenched. As soon as our hands touch new creation, we begin to whisper and pray our hopes and dreams. This transference is spiritual because our children live in hope until they recognize the misfortunes of the world. These misfortunes become the cornerstone of hope as we explain away the ills of society. God is our hope.

The pieces in this section speak to our unwillingness to surrender to defeat. Our pursuit to triumph over our enemies in the face of surpassing odds. Our quest for the things of God. Our positioning ourselves for the future and for our loved ones. Words have long been our weapons of hope in the face of danger and uncertainty. Hear these words of hope.

Women of color hope because deep in their souls are the expectations of a life that God has designed for them. This life is free from sexual, racial, or class limitations and bears the imprint of God's touch through God's spirit. It is through the spirit of God that women of color are set free!

GOOD NEWS

Those who have died have never never left
The dead have a pact with the living
They are in the woman's breast
They are in the wailing child
They are with us in the home
They are with us in the crowd
The dead have a pact with the living

Sweet Honey in the Rock

WEDDING SERMON OF THE REVEREND SENIOR PULLIAM

There is nothing in nature like [love].... Love is divine only and difficult always. If you think it is easy you are a fool. If you think it is natural you are blind. It is a learned application without reason or motive except that it is God.

You do not deserve love regardless of the suffering you have endured. You do not deserve love because somebody did you wrong. You do not deserve love just because you want it. You can only earn—by practice and careful contemplation—the right to express it and you have to learn how to accept it. Which is to say you have to earn God. You have to practice God ... Love is not a gift. It is a diploma. A diploma conferring certain privileges: the privilege of expressing love and the privilege of receiving it.

How do you know you have graduated? You don't. What you do know is that you are human and therefore educable, and therefore capable of learning how to learn, and therefore interesting to God, who is interested only in Himself which is to say He is interested only in love. Do you understand me? God is not interested in you. He is interested in love and that bliss it brings to those who understand and share that interest.

Couples that enter the sacrament of marriage and are not prepared to go the distance or are not willing to get right with the real love of God cannot thrive. They may cleave together like robins or gulls or anything else that mates for life. But if they eschew this mighty course, at the moment when all are judged for the disposition of their eternal lives, their cleaving won't mean a thing. God bless the pure and holy. Amen.

Toni Morrison

O Lord my God!

Instruct my ignorance and enlighten my Darkness.

Thou art my King, take [thou] the entire possession of [all] my powers and faculties and let me be no longer under the dominion of sin.

Give me a sincere and hearty repentance for all my [many] offences and strengthen by thy grace my resolutions on amendment and circumspection for the time to come. Grant me [also] the spirit of Prayer and Suppli[cation] according to thy own most gracious Promises.

Phillis Wheatley

Our Father who is the ruler of the Heavens, all
  knowing, all powerful, all present.
Thy name is holy and just, deserving of the praise
  most high.
My daily nourishment is in you, supplier of my
  need, fulfiller of my every desire.
Lead me along the path of righteous thinking,
  knowing there is nothing in opposition to you.
Your kingdom is the point of my ascension.
My daily communion draws me closer to your
  image and likeness, and as I become one in
  the One, my realization of this vast knowing
  simply is, and is all there is. Amen.

Gewreka Nobles

MY JOY

My Joy—
My Longing—
My Sanctuary—
My Friend—
My Food for the Journey—
My Final End—
You are my Spirit and my Hope.
You are my Yearning.
You are all my Good.

Rabi'a Al-Adawiyya

Dear God, I thank You for the gift of this child to raise, this life to share, this mind to help mold, this body to nurture, and this spirit to enrich.

Let me never betray this child's trust, dampen this child's hope, or discourage this child's dreams.

Help me, dear God, to help this precious child become all You mean him to be.

Let Your grace and love fall on him like gentle breezes and give him inner strength and peace and patience for the journey ahead.

Marian Wright Edelman

Each moment is magical, precious and complete and will never exist again.

Susan L. Taylor

YOU ARE SUFFICIENT

O my Lord,
Whatever you have apportioned to me of the
    worldly things
Give it all to my enemies.
And whatever you have apportioned to me in the
    world to come,
Give that to my friends.
For you are sufficient for me.

Rabi'a Al-Adawiyya

BORN AGAIN

Hallelujah!
I've been born again.
I've got a new walk
A new talk
A new song in my heart.
No more sickness
No more fear
No more worry.
By the grace of God
I am saved.
I have arrived
In all my glory.
I've come this far by faith.
I've got a new life
A new vision
A new home in Zion.
My soul has been renewed.
The Truth has set me free.
I am alive
Whole

Unlimited
Good.
I am Spirit
Woman
Friend
Lover
Teacher
Student
Artist
I wouldn't take nothin' for my journey now.
I've been born again
And this time
I'm ready for the world.
I've got a new walk
A new talk
A new song in my heart:
This little light of mine
I'm gonna let it shine
Let it shine
Let it shine
Let it shine.

Tawnicia Ferguson Rowan

BLESSED BE THE NEW YEAR

O Great Spirit of Hope, blessed be your holy
seasons,
Blessed be this season when we move to a new
year.
Blessed be this magical time for new beginnings
and fond farewells.
Blessed be this "crack between the worlds" that
we encounter at the New Year.
Blessed be this threshold place of transition
between inside and outside.
Blessed be this transformation when spirits of
hope and change gather.
Blessed be this passage from past securities to
uncharted uncertainties.
Blessed be this shifting of emotions.
Blessed be this letting go of old hurts and pains.
Blessed be this reliable balancing act of nature.
Blessed be this rededication of values and
meaning in life.

Blessed be ... (add others)
O Great Spirit of Hope, blessed be your holy
   seasons.

Diann L. Neu

LUCKY

The baby brought us luck
from the day we brought him home.
White curtains lifted
to let in the pale lemon light.
We hung his hat on the doorknob
and raised a flag
in the shape of a fish.
The man selling corn,
the woman folding sheets,
smiled and waved their approval.
The nurse left a poem in the mailbox.
Those who visited tiptoed around
the light that had landed in our living room.
The drunk declined his usual drink.
The lady with the many bracelets
stopped her jangling in mid-gesture.
It was as if they were entering a church.
We succumbed to sleep,
the three of us and slept
through the long mornings cool

with magnolias opening beneath our window.
His small hand curled around my thumb.
When I opened his rosebud fist, I found,
already etched, a complex map of his future.
My breasts were sweet for days.
The smell of milk
enticed a trail of black ants
to migrate out of the Boston fern.
Like a moving signature
weaving across the carpet,
it was his first alphabet.

Cathy Song

PRAYER FOR MY SONS

Holy Father, how I praise and magnify your holy name! I know that you are worthy of all honor and praise, for you have been faithful to me and to my family all our lives. I confess that we have not always been faithful to you, but you have forgiven and blessed us in spite of ourselves and I thank you.

Father, I present my sons to you. I ask that they will grow up whole, for whole is holy. I want them to be of a mind to praise you, to love you, to worship and adore you, for as long as you are primary in their lives, they will be strong, responsible Black men who are blessed to be a blessing.

Thank you, Father, for hearing your servant's prayer that is prayed in the precious name of my Lord and Savior, Jesus Christ. Amen.

Marjorie L. Kimbrough

The Lord is my shepherd, I shall not want.
He makes me lie down in green pastures;
he leads me beside still waters
he restores my soul.
He leads me in right paths
for his name's sake.

Even though I walk through the darkest valley,
I fear no evil;
for you are with me;
your rod and your staff—
they comfort me.

You prepare a table before me
in the presence of my enemies;
you anoint my head with oil;
my cup overflows.
Surely goodness and mercy shall follow me
all the days of my life,
and I shall dwell in the house of the Lord
my whole life long.

Psalm 23

All but overwhelmed by ubiquitous redefinitions of ourselves and our sense of reality, one tries to write. To think. To get some kind of clarity about almost anything. One tries to function. To stay sober, to stay connected with the deeper stratum of being that is one's identity, one's tradition, one's very perception and consciousness. All too often, one gives up. Drops out of school. Flunks too many courses. Quits too many jobs. Gives in to all-pervading despair, to the murderous thoughts the white world projects daily, hourly, year after year. One gives up and lies down and dies. Meanwhile, there seems little to do but to keep on keepin' on as the saying goes. One writes, thinks, works, talks, hopes against hope that the horror of white-think will somehow be turned around, that white madness can be cured. (White is used here to denote a mind-set or system of mental processes rather than a racial or genetic term. There are many

Caucasian people and communities who in the past and at present are as distant from "white-think" as any traditional Native American.)

Paula Gunn Allen

WITHOUT YOU

Without You, O my life, O my love,
I would never have wandered
Across these endless countries,
How many gifts and graces You have given me!
How many favors You have fed me from your
    hand!
I look for your love in all directions
Then suddenly its blessing burns in me.
O captain of my heart—
Radiant eye of longing in my breast—
I will never be free of You as long as I live.
Only be satisfied with me,
Life of my heart,
And I am satisfied.

Rabi'a Al-Adawiyya

4

HEALING

There is absolutely nothing like the virtue that flows from a woman. Yet the virtue of a healed woman transforms death itself. Women of color rise daily from spiritual death experiences that seek to destroy the soul—such as hopelessness, poverty, and addiction—to transform reality, and the world as we once knew it never exists again. The pain of our existence is expressed in lyrics, poetry, and prayer. Daily we need a touch from God that soothes our wounds and mends the broken areas of our lives. Women of color pray not just for ourselves but for the world. Our touch makes sore spots less tender. Our embrace suddenly mends fragmented souls. Our voice erases insults and persecution. Our smile blinds mean looks and hateful stares. Our godliness makes us appear taller than any mountain.

This collection of pieces bears witness to our ability to transform the world around us from a state of pain and confusion to one of order and peace. Prayer is a balm that heals. It soothes unarticulated fears and suppressed memories too painful to recollect. Our world is changed and renewed each morning, and women of color must assert the authority of our gift of healing to soothe the wounds of our people. The wounds are visible in the streets of urban America, in offspring abandoned and flung into a system that's not designed to protect them. The wounds can be felt in the aborted hopes and dreams of our sons drunk from depression and frustration. The wounds can be tasted in the bitterness of our daughters. Women of color must be active agents of healing.

MARIELA

One day you forget his bitter smell
and one day you forget your shame.
You remember how your small cry
rose like a blackbird from the corn,
when you picked yourself up from the earth
how the clouds moved on.

Sandra Cisneros

What we give to the poor, we lend to the Lord.

Sojourner Truth

MY WICKED WICKED WAYS

This is my father.
See? He is young.
He looks like Errol Flynn.
He is wearing a hat
that tips over one eye,
a suit that fits him good,
and baggy pants.
He is also wearing
those awful shoes,
the two-toned ones
my mother hates.

Here is my mother.
She is not crying.
She cannot look into the lens
because the sun is bright.
The woman,
the one my father knows,
is not here.
She does not come till later.

My mother will get very mad.
Her face will turn red
and she will throw one shoe.
My father will say nothing.
After a while everyone
will forget it.
Years and years will pass.
My mother will stop mentioning it.
This is me she is carrying
I am a baby.
She does not know
I will turn out bad.

Sandra Cisneros

Father/Mother God of us all
Who resides within us all
Your name is divine
Your presence is universal
Your spirit is manifested in and through us.
All our needs are satisfied
We release ourselves from self-made bondage
As we release others.
For Your kingdom is the only reality
And the only power throughout eternity. So it is.

Una Samms, Maureen Shaw, and Bev Spencer

AGAINST DOMESTIC VIOLENCE

Lord, many are in destructive marriages, yet wish to state, as Your Word suggests: "Til death do us part."

Thank you, Lord, for granting us the spiritual discernment to know that You did not mean only the death of one's body, but also the death of one's spirit, and even the death of the contract. As Nicodemus came to know, one does not have to re-enter his mother's womb to be born again, and neither does one have to die a physical death to be dead.

Give those who are being abused the strength needed to stand up to the abuser or give them the courage to leave. Grant the abusers Your grace and mercy. Draw them closer to You, that persons may find spiritual nourishment for empty souls. In Christ's name, we pray. Amen.

Rev. Chestina Mitchell Archibald

A HYMN FOR DADDY

This is not an elegy.
It is not sad, forlorn, or wistful.
It harbors no pain, no longing, and no regret.
It speaks not of loss, heartache, or missed
    opportunity.

This is not an elegy.
It is a song of celebration, in honor of a great soul
    whose work in this life is completed.
It is a loving tribute to the beauty of your smile,
    the passion in your eyes, and the generosity
    of your spirit.
It is a reflection on the precious time shared
    between a devoted father and your adoring
    daughter.

This is not an elegy.
It is the remembering of sing-alongs on the living
    room floor, piggy-back rides at parades, and
    kites rescued from trees.

It is the revisiting of piano recitals, cotillions,
    graduations, and the wedding of my dreams.
It is a retrospective appreciation for unbearable
    driving lessons, impossible curfews, and
    dissuaded suitors.

This is not an elegy.
It is a humble token of gratitude for the love,
    inspiration, and security I've always known.
It is a prayer that you have found even greater
    comforts and joys than those you have
    afforded me.
It is a hymn of praise and thanksgiving from a
    baby girl for a priceless gift—her Daddy.

Amen.

Tawnicia Ferguson Rowan

We know that this world is filled with discordant notes, but help us, Father, to so unite our efforts that we may all join in one harmonious symphony for peace and brotherhood, justice and equality of opportunity for all men.

The tasks performed today with forgiveness for all our errors, we dedicate, Dear Lord, to Thee. Grant us strength and courage and faith and humility sufficient for the tasks assigned to us.

Mary McLeod Bethune

MEMBERSHIP

I shall not die without leaving children behind.
I shall not die empty-handed.

Anonymous African woman

KINDRED SPIRITS FROM DIFFERENT PLACES

I see it in your eyes and God does too
I feel it in your pain and God does too
It screams past your silence yet is so audible to
    God
Undeserved suffering,
prolonged frustration,
shattered hope have become your resting place
Yet in a little while God will undo the past and
    make right your future
Live in Hope it conquers defeat
Pray in Faith it destroys the impossible
Love with your Heart for it is pure
Rest in God's promise for your today.

Christal M. Jackson

MY SHATTERED SISTER

Sister, I wish to be the waters
of insistent rivers
the long arms of the Colorado
that reach past those man-made borders
to the surging Amazon currents.
Is not your blood my blood
whether coursing through veins
of family I have never met
or spilled on the land
of a continent we share?
My blood is yours,
we are the bleeding twins.
You are the Southern sister
veiled in oppressive shadow
that covers your enigmatic light,
I, the Northern twin,
watch angrily
with fists clenched tight
the cancer that invades
our ancestors' defiled dreams.

Your cries become deafening
as the distance disappears.
Deserts burn,
jungles part silent,
your broken body
appears before me
in a paid advertisement
on the 11 o'clock news
as you break the zombie stupor
of televised distraction.
You are the drumming noise
of my sleepless nights.
The dancing voices of children
become a mother's anguished cries
and ricochet off
the prefabricated fortresses
we have so carefully constructed.
You haunt me sister
when I pretend
it could never happen here
or as I turn the pages
and read the countless headlines:
Latino family of 12 living in a 2-room shack,
Health care denied campesinos,
Latino unemployment doubles.
Somewhere a warm wind whirls

past our neon-lit hopes,
it is your breath sister
carrying the scent
of ashes and blood
as your voice becomes the river
that connects us.
And we all walk quieter in the clutches of the
     North
when we hear the splintered echoes
of America to the South.

Naomi Quinonez

Love gives itself away.
In fact, love is not love until it is given away.

Della Reese

CHANT FOR A SICK CHILD

Mother: O spirits of our ancestors, this little one I hold is my child. She is your child also. Be good to her.

Women: She has entered a world of trouble. There is sickness. There is cold and pain. The pain that you knew when you were here, the sickness with which you are familiar.

Mother: Let her sleep in peace. For there is healing in sleep. Let her be healed. Let no one have anger toward us.

Women: O spirits of the past, let her grow. Let her be strong. Let her become a woman. Then she will offer a sacrifice to you that will fill your hearts with delight.

Pygmy women

The mother recites her part of the prayer, holding her sick child. The other women respond as a chorus, chanting.

Our never-ending Source of all, Your very
nature is divine.
Life is in perfect harmony.
We have aligned our consciousness with You, our
never-ending Source.
Every day we partake of Your substance.
We eliminate our error thoughts about ourselves,
and about others.
Let us never manifest separation, which comes
from the illusion of duality.
Take us to the place where we know there is only
You, God. Amen.

Virginia Clemons, Nerissa Street,
and Sharon Yamamoto

PEACE ON EARTH

How can we have peace in the Middle East
When there's none at home?
How can we have understanding in the land
When there's none in the woman and there's
    none in the man?

How can we heal the wounds of the world
If we cannot heal our own?
And where does this peace on earth begin
If not in the home?

Where do we go now?
Do we let the devil win?
Or do we get up and fight?
Surely we know how to conquer all fear
Bring an end to the violence
Bring an end to the tears

Well there's too much talk about it
And too many walk without it

Where is the love?
Where is the God in your life?
To my left a woman abuses her children
To my right somebody's beating his wife
Tell me, where is the love?!!
Where is the God in your life?!!

How can we heal the wounds of the world
If we cannot heal our own?
And where does this peace on earth begin
If not in the home?

Rachelle Ferrell

IN DESPERATION OF GRIEF

My husband, you have abandoned me.
My husband is gone, and will never return.
I am lost. Where will I go?
You used to fetch water for me. You collected the
    firewood.
You clothed me and fed me with good things.
Why have you left me? Why have you done this
    to me?
Where will I go?

Ashanti women's wailing prayer, Ghana

HE'S ALWAYS THERE (Matthew 28:20)

He's always there
To brighten up your day
Always there in every way
When it's cold and dreary
And your faith is growing weary
You don't have to be afraid
He's always there
Just ask for what you need
He'll be there if you believe
Open up your heart
Invite him to come in
He'll turn your life around
And change you from within
Waiting to care
He's always there
He's always there
To comfort and provide
He's always there right by your side
To help you face tomorrow
Through all the joy and sorrow

His love you can't deny
He's always there
Just ask for what you need
He'll be there if you believe
Open up your heart
Invite him to come in
He'll turn your life around
And he'll change you from within
Waiting to care
He's always there

CeCe Winans and Madeline Stone

Just as crying is the only manner of expression a child uses to let its wishes be known — be it hunger, thirst or pain — in the beginning stages of spirituality you have only one way of expressing your heart, and that is through shedding tears of intense longing.

The Master will bind you with his [her] love and he [she] will become the absolute center of your life. Awakening to our deepest desires, to our needs and to our truth requires reflection and inner listening. We must create space in our lives where our physical self and our spiritual being can meet. The more we nourish our internal world, the more powerful we grow in the external world.

Susan L. Taylor

O Lord, when I meditate upon the wisdom of Your conduct among your creatures, I perceive that Your justice crushes them.

Then I reflected upon myself by the vastness of Your mercy and realized that Your effusive grace embraces every being.

O Lord, You have delayed chastisement of sinners, so Your lack of haste and granting of respite to them has made them desirous of Your gracious forgiveness.

And why should it not be like this, since your bounty and grace towards previous peoples and nations was equally generous.

Anonymous Sufi woman, Arjan

MOURNING A SISTER'S DEATH

When your sister first dies
Do you say
She was or is my sister
He is or was my sister's child
Erlinda, saying your name sounds rough
Like the life you lived:
You led street gangs
Smoked
And didn't go to school
When others did
You've left children
Rough and lost like you
Scattered children
Like you were scattered —
No one wants them, has time for them
Like they didn't want
Or have time for you
"What will happen to her children,"
"What happened to Erlinda,"
Mourners asked

She died an alcoholic
Displaced from rural birth
And transplanted in an urban setting
Caught in a gringo world —
Once beautiful
She died amongst the junkies
Pimps and whores
Of the asphalt city.

Irene I. Blea

LET ONE REMAIN

O Mother Who Lives in the Spirit Land, we offer you these bananas and eggs. Receive them and eat. We thank you very much that you allowed this child to come to us, and we beg you to send another.

And you, infant who has left, receive these eggs. They are yours. Now give back to your mother, saying, "Let one come to her again, but this time permit it to remain."

Ashanti women, Ghana

This prayer comes from a sacred ritual performed by Ashanti women when a baby who is less than a week old dies. The infant's mother and her own mother bring eggs and mashed bananas or yams to a crossroads, where the prayer is offered.

5

COURAGE

Despite the terror in our hearts, we manage to make our enemies flee. Not because we're unafraid, but because we understand we can't afford to be afraid. Women of color treat fear like a mean neighbor, an estranged friend, or a bitter relative, showing it just enough attention to force it to respond to our voice, and we win. How do we manage to be so brave? Just where does this strength come from? Women of color know that we must be courageous because someone is watching. Not our enemy, but our sons and daughters who rely on our strength.

Our courage distracts our opposition, and while we have captured their attention, our ability to demonstrate courage weakens them. Our weapons aren't visible to the naked eye but are like fierce darts of fire that consume anything that attempts to deter or destroy our beloved. This fire is fierce because it is created by God deep in our soul. We don't fully understand it because we too are amazed by its ever-present power in any situation. Courage is called to face the enemy of freedom, which is fear. The pieces in this collection reflect the power of courage in women of color. Listen to our voices.

Once African American women begin to use spiritual power as a political force, creativity opens. Spirituality can then become for us and, I believe, for everyone who uses it in this conscious and responsible way, an extremely rich source for the creative.

Akasha Gloria Hull

DARKNESS

You created me in darkness and then
You draped my soul with it.
Darkness no longer frightens me.
It is the place of
my inner creation
that equips me to imagine,
thrive,
conquer,
achieve,
and love.

Christal M. Jackson

A CHILD'S PRAYER

Daddy, who hangs out way upstairs, your very
name warms my heart.

All that You are I share, all that You wish for me,
I summon, just like it happens up where You
are.

So let it be here as it is there.

Provide for me in this present moment with Your
bountiful blessings.

Cancel what I owe, as I cancel what is owed to
me.

Hide and protect me from what is not from You.

For You are everything that is, was, and is to
become. Amen.

Helen Macbeth

IT'S ALL WITHIN ME

Why should I tremble or withdraw in shame
When I am God's child, and I AM is my name?

Why would I wrestle with sorrow or fear
When God's love and protection are nearer than
near?

Why would I wonder at time or at space
Or marvel at wisdom, and beauty, and grace?

Why would I long for more courage or power
Or question my instincts from hour to hour?

Why would I feel insufficient or small
Or believe that I'm unfit to answer God's call?

Why, when I AM is creative and bold
Would I shrink from Its light, instead of unfold?

Why, when I know that my God is my guide
Would I pause to consider keeping It inside?

Why would I think that I lack anything
When the Lord is my God, and my Source, and
    my King?

Why, when God's face is in all that I see
Would I keep on forgetting, *It's all within me?!*

Tawnicia Ferguson Rowan

MY DESIRE

To reach the unreachable
To touch those no one wants to touch
To find the lost ones
And tell them why you love them so much
My desire is to be a vessel, Lord
My desire is to be a vessel, Lord
To go where some dare not go
To tread in places without paths
To be a light in darkness
Your power, Lord, is what I need to have
For You said if I desire any good thing, it would
    come to pass
Lord, I want a ministry that will last
My desire is to be a vessel, Lord
My desire is to be a vessel, Lord
To do the unthinkable
When everyone around me wants to doubt
To accomplish the impossible
Your power will bring me out

You said if I desire any good thing, it would come
   to pass
Lord I want a ministry, to touch all people, that
   will last.

My desire is to be a vessel, Lord
My desire is to be a vessel, Lord

Yolanda Adams

Life is a journey back to God, and our relationships are the road we travel.

Susan L. Taylor

THE HISTORY OF FIRE

My mother is a fire beneath a stone.
My father, lava.
My grandmother is a match,
My sister straw.
Grandfather is kindling like trees of the world.
My brothers are gunpowder,
And I am smoke with gray hair,
Ash with black fingers and palms.
I am wind for the fire.
My dear one is a jar of burned bones
I have saved.
This is where our living goes
And still we breathe,
And even the dry grass
With sun and lightning above it
Has no choice but to grow
And then lie down
With no other end in sight.
Air is between these words,
Fanning the flame.

Linda Hogan

O God, let fear die and conviction be born in
    our lives.
Let Your light dawn in our minds as the day
    dawns on the earth.
Let us not be so busy hurrying into the future
    and
Worrying about the past that we lose
Today—the only one we have.
God, help us do what we know we have to do
    today,
And leave tomorrow to You.

Marian Wright Edelman

Look to the light within you. It's awaiting your attention, longing for your return. You may have lost sight of your *inner radiance* as you turned to look outside yourself for validation and meaning. You may have forgotten it as you gave authority not to your own inner voice, but to the dictates and opinions of others. Yet no matter how far you wander or how long you stay away, the *divine light* never flickers or dims. You are host to the eternal flame. It glows in the silence of your being to illumine your life and light your way.

Susan L. Taylor

O God, go with my child as he goes to college
Keep him safe
Keep him sensible
Keep him focused
Keep him joyful
Keep him surrounded by friends and teachers
     who help him grow.

Help him not to succumb to alcohol or other
     drugs
To the fast crowd going nowhere
To the lure of laziness or the glamour of cliques
To careless sex and careless habits
But to be his own person and avoid group-think.

Help me to write more and call less!
To know I miss him
To feel my prayers and remember his home
Teachings
To visit home as often as he can and know it

Remains a place where reservations are never
Needed and no locks will ever bar his return.

Help him always to remember how much I love
him.

Marian Wright Edelman

The Black Hills have great significance to the Lakota and Dakota people. It is said that the prayer of the white man, the Lord's prayer, has meaning because the Black Hills is on earth as it is in heaven. It mirrors the constellations.

Patricia Locke

To really live is to grow
To grow is to change.
When we let go and let God,
we will grow through the change,
and we will be successful.
The death of the old is the birth of new.

Della Reese

For as matters stand presently, Native people are uneasy knowing that if we fail to live in accordance with the false identity foisted off on us to the satisfaction of the powerful white world, we will again be consigned to the outer darkness of poverty, disease, and hopelessness. The threat is very real, and the mindlessness, the culture-wide delusion that occasions it, is very dangerous to those of us who live in accordance with another view of the nature of reality and of the role of human consciousness within it.

Paula Gunn Allen

PARENT PLEAS

O God, my child is addicted to drugs and alcohol and I don't want anybody to know. Tell me what to do. Give me the strength to cope.

O God, my child has AIDS and I'm so afraid. Tell me how to help. Give me the strength to cope.

O God, my father abused me as a child and my secret eats away at me every day. Tell me where to seek help. Give me the strength to cope.

O God, my child has run away from home and I don't know where she is. Send her home and heal our rift. Give me the strength to cope.

O God, my child has joined a gang and dances with danger. Show me how to respond. Give me the strength to cope.

O God, my child is out of control. I am out of control and my life is out of control. Give me the strength to cope.

Only Your holy presence can make us well again.

Marian Wright Edelman

BREAKING TRADITION

for my daughter

My daughter denies she is like me,
Her secretive eyes avoid mine.
She reveals the hatreds of womanhood
already veiled behind music and smoke and
    telephones.
I want to tell her about the empty room
of myself.
This room we lock ourselves in
where whispers live like fungus,
giggles about small breasts and cellulite,
where we confine ourselves to jealousies,
bedridden by menstruation.
This waiting room where we feel our hands
are useless, dead speechless clamps
that need hospitals and forceps and kitchens
and plugs and ironing boards to make them
    useful.
I deny I am like my mother. I remember why:

She kept her room neat with silence,
defiance smothered in requirements to be
    otonashii,
passion and loudness wrapped in an obi,
her steps confined to ceremony,
the weight of her sacrifice she carried like
a fetus. Guilt passed on in our bones.
I want to break tradition—unlock this room
where women dress in the dark.
Discover the lies my mother told me.
The lies that we are small and powerless
that our possibilities must be compressed
to the size of pearls, displayed only as
passive chokers, charms around our neck.
Break Tradition
I want to tell my daughter of this room of myself
filled with tears of violins,
the light in my hands,
poems about madness,
the music of yellow guitars—
sounds shaken from barbed wire and
goodbyes and miracles of survival.
This room of open windows where daring ones
    escape.
My daughter denies she is like me

her secretive eyes are walls of smoke
and music and telephones,
her pouting ruby lips, her skirts
swaying to salsa, teena marie and the stones,
her thighs displayed in carnivals of color.
I do not know the contents of her room.
She mirrors my aging.
She is breaking tradition.

Janice Mirikitani

Passion and purpose fuel your wants, propel your dreams into action. *Together,* they fire you up and motivate you to claim your destiny.

Monique Greenwood

LET ME REMEMBER

Wherever *I am God is*,
Fear wears many faces,
If it is not love, it is fear.
Love will overshadow fear.
The light of truth will overshadow fear.
While I embrace fear, it becomes my ally.
False Expectations Appearing Real are not the
    truth.
Faith will starve fear.

Iyanla Vanzant

Dear God, in the Glorious
name of Jesus
I do now and
for the rest of my life
renounce every idea
 every idea
 every endeavor
 every appetite and value
which does not conform
to your specific purpose
for my life.
I resolve to know you
to seek you
to bless you
that You Lord will get the Glory
out of my Life.
Amen

Rev. Dr. Cecelia Williams Bryant

Remember your birth, how your mother
    struggled
to give you form and breath. You are evidence of
her life, and her mother's, and hers.
Remember your father, his hands cradling
your mother's flesh, and maybe her heart too
and maybe not.
He is your life also.

Joy Harjo

From beyond time,
beyond oak trees and bright clever water flow,
she was given the work of weaving the strands
of her body, her pain, her vision
into creation, and the gift of having created, to
    disappear.

Paula Gunn Allen

MY MOTHER PIECED QUILTS

They were just meant as covers
In winters
As weapons
Against pounding January winds
But it was just that every morning I awoke to
     these
October ripened canvases
Passed my hand across their cloth faces
And began to wonder how you pieced
All these together
These strips of gentle communion cotton and
     flannel
Nightgowns
Wedding organdies
Dime-store velvets
How you shaped patterns square and oblong and
     round
Positioned
Balanced
Then cemented them

With your thread
A steel needle
A thimble
How the thread darted in and out
Galloping along the frayed edges, tucking
    them in
As you did us at night
Oh how you stretched and turned and
    rearranged
Your Michigan spring faded curtain pieces
My father's Santa Fe workshirt
The summer denims, the tweeds of fall
In the evening you sat at your canvas
—our cracked linoleum floor the drawing board
Me lounging on your arm
And you staking out the plan:
Whether to put the lilac purple of Easter
    against the
Red plaid of winter-going-into-spring
Whether to mix a yellow with a blue and white
    and paint
The Corpus Christi noon when my father held
    your hand
Whether to shape a five-point star from the
Somber black silk you wore to grandmother's
    funeral

You were the river current
Carrying the roaring notes
Forming them into pictures of a little boy
    reclining
A swallow flying
You were the caravan master at the reins
Driving your threaded needle artillery across the
Mosaic cloth bridges
Delivering yourself in separate testimonies
O mother you plunged me sobbing and laughing
Into our past
Into the river crossing at five
Into the spinach fields
Into the plainview cotton rows
Into tuberculosis wards
Into braids and muslin dresses
Sewn hard and taut to withstand the thrashings
Of twenty-five years
Stretched out they lay
Armed/ready/shouting/celebrating
Knotted with love
The quilts sing on

Teresa Palomo Acosta

TRUST

God, so many times I've trusted you in the face of great danger, despair, confusion, anguish, rejection and grief but your presence never failed to sustain me. You kept me through the valley of the shadow of death and you never let my enemies put me to shame.

Oh, how I trust you.

In the midst of abandonment and betrayal you hid me under the shadow of your wings. When my life took a course that I didn't fully understand as a result of your leading, you led me to a wide space and made my feet like that of a deer.

Yes, God, I trust you.

In the midst of uncovering the mystery of my creation as a woman who knew too well the experiences of racism, sexism, and classism, you always managed to make room for me that defied the natural laws of humankind's understanding.

For that, God, I trust you.

Even when my faith is tested and my pathway is not clear, I'm reminded that you will never leave or forsake me. When your voice commands me to stretch beyond where I am, I yield in pursuit of a higher calling. Thanks for always using my struggles to strengthen me.

I truly trust you.

You are my hope, my life source, my joy, my everything, and yet will I trust YOU!

Amen!

Christal M. Jackson

About the Contributors

Acosta, Teresa Palomo Acosta is a Chicana poet whose collection of poems titled *Nile & Other Poems* appeared in 1999. She was formerly a research associate with the Texas State Historical Association and is the coauthor of *Las Tejanas: 300 Years of History,* published by the University of Texas Press in 2003. She lives in Austin.

Adams, Yolanda An acclaimed singer of gospel-themed R&B music, Adams won a Grammy Award in 1999 for her album *Mountain High ... Valley Low*, after being nominated for a Grammy in 1996 for a live album. Formerly a schoolteacher in Houston, she released her debut album *Just As I Am* in 1988 on the Sounds of Gospel label. Her most recent popular album is *Believe*, released in 2001.

Al-Adawiyya, Rabi'a A Sufi saint and mystic, Al-Adawiyya is believed to have lived from 717 to 801 CE in Basra, now in Iraq. As a poor orphan she was sold into slavery. Later she was freed by her master after he saw her absorbed in prayer, a light miraculously appearing over her head that illuminated the entire house. Once freed, she moved to the desert, where she devoted herself to prayer.

Allen, Paula Gunn Of Laguna, Sioux, and Lebanese ancestry, Allen is a poet, novelist, and critic. She obtained her PhD at the University of New Mexico in 1976 and has had a notable academic career in documenting and teaching Native American traditions and literature. She has taught at Fort Lewis College, Durango, Colorado; the College of San Mateo; San Diego State University; San Francisco State University, where she was the director of the Native American Studies Program; the University of New Mexico, Albuquerque; and the University of California at Berkeley, where she was professor of Native American/ethnic studies. She retired from her position as professor of English/creative writing/American Indian studies at the University of California at Los Angeles in 1999. Among her books are *The Sacred Hoop: Recovering the Feminine in American Indian Traditions; Spider Woman's Granddaughters;* and *Grandmothers of the Light.*

Archibald, Rev. Chestina Mitchell Rev. Archibald is a nationally renowned minister and educator who is chaplain-in-residence at Fisk University. A former member of the editorial board for *Gospel Today* magazine and a writer for the national Baptist Publishing board, she lives in Nashville, Tennessee. She is the author of *Say Amen! The African American Family's Book of Prayers* and *The Secrets of the Psalms.*

Bess, Savitri L. A transpersonal therapist, workshop facilitator, and fiber artist who was awarded a Fulbright and a National Endowment for the Arts grant, Bess has been on the path of the Divine Mother for more than twenty-seven years. Her book *The Path of the Mother* is the story of one woman's journey from desolation to spiritual wholeness, a road map for making contact with the Divine Feminine as well as a portrait of Ammachi, a living Hindu saint.

Bethune, Mary McLeod (1875–1955) One of seventeen children of former slaves, Bethune rose from childhood poverty in South Carolina to become a leading black educator. She founded a school for African American girls in Daytona, Florida, which later became Bethune-Cookman College. She also founded the National Council of Negro Women and was a vice president of the National Association for the

Advancement of Colored People. She served as an advisor on African American issues for President Franklin Roosevelt and as an advisor on race relations for the United Nations.

Blea, Irene I. Blea is an author, sociologist, and researcher who has long been active in the gender and racial equality movements in the United States. She is a professor, a poet, a consultant, and a spiritual counselor to those confronting contradictions in a materialistic, multicultural society. She is the author most recently of *The Feminization of Racism: Promoting World Peace in America; La Chicana and the Intersection of Race, Class, and Gender*; and *U.S. Chicanas and Latinas within a Global Context*.

Bryant, Rev. Dr. Cecelia Williams The Episcopal supervisor of the Fifth Episcopal District of the African Methodist Episcopal Church, Rev. Dr. Bryant is the founder and spiritual director of Akousa Visions, a global ministry for African diasporic women, and the founder of the African Methodist Episcopal Church in Cote D'Ivoire. She is the author of *Kiamsha: A Spiritual Discipline for African American Women*. She received the Women Who Dare Award from the National Black Women's Health Project.

Cisneros, Sandra A novelist, short-story writer, essayist, and poet, Cisneros is one of the first Latina American writers to achieve commercial success. She is best known for her novel *The House on Mango Street* and several poetry collections, including *My Wicked Wicked Ways*. She is praised by scholars and critics for works that help bring the perspective of Chicana women into the mainstream of literary feminism. Her recent novel is *Caramelo*, the saga of a Mexican American family.

De Veaux, Masani Alexis A writer, poet, playwright, and educator, De Veaux was raised in New York City and given her African name, Masani, by a South African friend in 1986. Writing as Alexis De Veaux, she published an acclaimed 2004 biography of Audre Lorde titled *Warrior Poet*, as well as several plays and a novel, *Spirits in the Street*. De Veaux currently teaches in the Department of Women's Studies at the University of Buffalo, where she earned her PhD.

Edelman, Marian Wright Founder and president of the Children's Defense Fund, which is widely considered to be the most effective national lobbying organization for children, Edelman is a writer and an attorney who has received numerous leadership awards. Active in the 1960s civil rights movement as a student and later staff attorney for the National Association for the Advancement of Colored People, she received a MacArthur Fellowship in 1985. She is the author of the national bestseller *The Measure of Our Success: Letter to My Children and Yours* and *Lantern: A Memoir of Mentors*, among many other books.

Ferrell, Rachelle A creative jazz vocalist as well as a classically trained musician, Ferrell has released several albums that have received critical and popular praise, including *Individuality (Can I Be Me?)*. Since the 1990s, she has been touring in Japan and Europe, as well as playing to full houses in American cities.

Greenwood, Monique Former editor-in-chief of *Essence* magazine, Greenwood is an author, businesswoman, and community leader. She left her editorial career to devote more time to her family and to develop her own businesses, which include Akwaaba Mansion, the nationally acclaimed bed and breakfast in Bedford-Stuyvesant, Brooklyn, the nearby restaurant Akwaaba Café, and Akwaaba by the Sea, a bed and breakfast in Cape May, New Jersey.

Harjo, Joy An enrolled member of the Muskogee Tribe, Harjo was born in Oklahoma. She is a writer, poet, artist, screenwriter, and musician, and has had her work published in *Massachusetts Review*, *Ploughshares*, *River Styx*, *Contact II*, *The Bloomsbury Review*, *Journal of Ethnic Studies*, *American Voice*, *Sonora Review*, *Kenyon Review*, *Beloit Poetry Review*, *Greenfield Review*, and *Puerto del Sol*. Her most recent musical album is *Native Joy for Real*. She lives and teaches in Hawaii.

Hogan, Linda A writer and professor of English whose tribal affiliation is Chickasaw, Hogan came from a military family that moved frequently, and thus she did not grow up within an Indian community, although most of her childhood was spent in Oklahoma and Colorado. She taught at the University of Colorado in Boulder, served on the National Endowment for the Arts poetry panel, and has been involved in wildlife rehabilitation as a volunteer. The main focus and movement of Hogan's work concerns the traditional indigenous view of and relationship to the land, animals, and plants.

Hull, Akasha Gloria A writer, poet, historian, and critic, Hull is the author of *Soul Talk: The New Spirituality of African American Women*, as well as volumes of poetry and prose. She has received fellowships from the Rockefeller Foundation, the National Endowment for the Humanities, the Ford Foundation, the Mellon Foundation, and the American Association of University Women. Since 1988, she has served as professor of women's studies and literature at the University of California, Santa Cruz.

Jackson, Christal M. Named one of "Thirty Leaders of the Future" by *Ebony* magazine in 1999, Jackson is the founder of Sisters with Wings, a nonprofit organization serving women and children, and a former intern with the Children's Defense Fund. She has an MA in theological studies from Duke University and lives in Houston.

Kimbrough, Marjorie L. The author of *Coffee Breaks of Faith*, *Everyday Miracles*, *Stories between the Testaments*, and *She Is Worthy*, Kimbrough is a contributor to *365 Meditations for Mothers of Teens* and *365 More Meditations for Women*. She lives in Atlanta.

Kudaka, Geraldine A filmmaker, poet, and writer, Kudaka was one of the founders of Third World Communications, editor of *Third World Women's Book*, and a poet-teacher for the Poetry in the Schools project. She has been published in numerous magazines and anthologies and is the author of *On a Bed of Rice*.

Locke, Patricia (1928–2001) A Hunkpapa Lakota and Chippewa of the Mississippi Bank, Locke lived on the Standing Rock Reservation in South Dakota and worked to preserve tribal languages and sacred

Indian sites. She was a MacArthur Fellow; executor of the International Native American Language Institute; chair of the American Indian Advisory Committee for the Martin Luther King Jr. Commission; and former president of the National Indian Education Association. As an educator, Locke taught at UCLA, San Francisco Valley State College, Alaska Methodist University, Denver University, the University of Colorado at Boulder, and the University of Southern Maine and was the author of many articles and publications.

Manyarrows, Victoria Lena A writer and photographer, Manyarrows was born in North Dakota and is of Tsalagi/Cherokee ancestry. She is the author of numerous books, including a volume of poetry called *Songs from the Native Lands*, as well as *Unsettling America* and *Skin Deep: Women Writing on Color, Culture and Identity*. She is a contributor to many multicultural and Native publications.

Mirikitani, Janice A third-generation Japanese American, Mirikitani is a poet, choreographer, teacher, and community organizer. She is program director of Glide Church/Urban Center, a multiracial and multicultural institution in San Francisco known for its social activism. As part of her responsibilities, she has created and directs an arts program that includes theater, dance, poetry, writing, and music. Her most recent volume of poetry is *Awake in the River*.

Morrison, Toni One of the most respected contemporary novelists, Morrison has portrayed the African American experience in many award-winning novels. An editor at Random House for many years, she was instrumental in getting the works of several young black writers published. Her novel *Song of Solomon* won the National Book Critics Circle award, and her fifth novel, *Beloved*, won a Pulitzer Prize in 1988. Morrison won the 1993 Nobel Prize for Literature and the National Book Foundation's Medal for Distinguished Contribution to American Letters. Her most recent novels have been *Paradise* and *Love*. She is a professor at Princeton University.

Neu, Diann L. Cofounder and codirector of the Women's Alliance for Theology, Ethics, and Ritual, in Silver Springs, Maryland, Neu is a feminist liturgist and licensed psychotherapist, holding both DMin and MSW degrees. Among her publications are *Return Blessings: Ecofeminist Liturgies Renewing the Earth* and *Women's Rites: Feminist Liturgies for Life's Journey*. She is also the author of *Peace Liturgies; Gathered at Sophia's Table: A Feminist Peace Seder; Women-Church Sourcebook;*

Women of Fire: A Pentecost Event; Women and the Gospel Traditions; Women-Church Celebrations; A Seder of the Sisters of Sarah; Miriam's Sisters Rejoice; and *Together at Freedom's Table.*

Quinonez, Naomi A poet and native of Los Angeles, Quinonez is widely published in anthologies and literary journals. Her first book of poetry was *Hummingbird Dream.* She coedited *Invocation L.A.: Urban Multicultural Poetry,* winner of a 1990 American Book Award. She teaches Chicano studies at the California State University in Fullerton.

Reese, Della A singer, actress, and ordained minister, Reese began her musical career as a child singing gospel music and was nominated for two Grammy Awards. She also starred in the hit television series *Touched by an Angel,* as well as numerous films and television shows. Reese is actively involved in diabetes awareness campaigns and is the founding minister of a nondenominational church in Los Angeles called "Understanding Principles for Better Living." Her autobiography is titled *Angels along the Way.*

Rowan, Tawnicia Ferguson The President and CEO of Well-Written Words, Inc., a South Florida–based freelance writing, editing, and consulting company,

Rowan is a passionate writer, educator, and scholar with a wealth of knowledge in her field. A published author with degrees in English literature from Spelman College and Vanderbilt University, Rowan has worked as a journalist, research assistant, writing consultant, and college professor. She and her husband, James, are active members of their church, the Universal Truth Center for Better Living, and self-professed "truth students" who believe that independent study, a sense of adventure, and a spirit of gratitude are the keys to a fulfilling life.

Song, Cathy A poet of Chinese heritage born in Hawaii, Song holds degrees from Wellesley College and Boston University. Her first book, *Picture Bride,* won the Yale Series of Younger Poets Award in 1982. *Frameless Windows, Squares of Light* was published in 1988, followed by *School Figures* and *The Land of Bliss.* She has been the recipient of the Hawaii Award for Literature and a National Endowment for the Arts fellowship. She lives in Honolulu.

Stone, Madeline A composer and pianist, Stone focuses her work on contemporary Christian music and gospel music. Her songs have been performed by many artists and groups, including CeCe Winans, Kathy Troccoli, and Anointed.

Sweet Honey in the Rock Founded in 1973 in Washington, D.C., by Dr. Bernice Johnson Reagon, Sweet Honey in the Rock is a Grammy Award–winning African American female a cappella ensemble with deep musical roots in the sacred music of the black church. The six-member group sings spirituals, hymns, gospel, jazz, and blues and has released numerous popular albums. After thirty years of leading and singing with the ensemble, Reagon retired from Sweet Honey in 2004. Her 1993 book, *We Who Believe in Freedom: Sweet Honey in the Rock Still on the Journey*, recounts the path of this group, whose members raise their voices in hope, love, justice, peace, and resistance.

Taylor, Susan L. The editor-in-chief of *Essence* magazine since 1981, Taylor is a writer and speaker who has inspired millions of readers through her column "In the Spirit" and her numerous public appearances. Her published books are *In the Spirit* and *Lessons in Living*. She lives in New York City.

Truth, Sojourner (c. 1797–1883) A preacher, abolitionist, and feminist, Truth was born into slavery in upstate

New York and fled to New York City when her master refused to acknowledge the abolition of slavery in the state in 1827. Her memoirs were published in 1878 as *The Narrative of Sojourner Truth*. She worked all her life for the rights of blacks and women.

Tubman, Harriet (c. 1821–1913) A fugitive slave and abolitionist who is best known for her work on the Underground Railroad, Tubman was born into slavery in Maryland. She escaped to freedom but returned to the South again and again to help free at least three hundred others. After the Civil War, she joined her family in Auburn, New York. Her story was first told in 1869 and published in 1886 as *Harriet Tubman: The Moses of Her People*.

Universal Foundation for Better Living Members of this New Thought Christian organization reinterpreted the Lord's Prayer into their own words on a spiritual retreat in 2002. Collaborative authors whose prayers appear in this book are Virginia Clemons, Norma Eaton, Wendy Gordon, Dr. Phyllis Green, Marcia Grubb, Helen Macbeth, Rev. Dr. Sheila McKeithen, Susan Newbold, Gewreka Nobles, Rev. Dr. Anna Price, Una Samms, Deborah Sharperson, Maureen Shaw, Bev Spencer, Nerissa Street, Cherlyn Taylor,

Rev. Dr. Mary Tumpkin, Jacqui Vanterpool, and Sharon Yamamoto.

Vanzant, Iyanla Vanzant is an award-winning and best-selling author of inspirational books, including *Acts of Faith, The Value in the Valley, Faith in the Valley,* and *In the Meantime.* She is an ordained minister and spiritual life counselor and lectures and facilitates workshops nationally with a mission to assist in the empowerment of women and men everywhere.

Wheatley, Phillis (c. 1753–1784) The first African American poet, Wheatley was brought to Boston on a slave ship when she was about eight years old. Purchased by a tailor named John Wheatley, she was taught to read and write and began writing poetry at age thirteen. In 1773, she was taken to England, where she became popular in society through her conversational skills. Her book *Poems on Various Subjects, Religious and Moral* was published in London that year. After returning to America, Wheatley was freed and married John Peters, a free black man. She died in poverty, and volumes of her memoirs and letters were published in 1834 and 1864.

Winans, CeCe A renowned vocalist and songwriter, Winans has won five Grammy Awards in the gospel music category and has released numerous albums, among them several gold and platinum bestsellers. She was born the eighth of ten siblings in the musical Winans family in Detroit. With various members of her family, she has recorded albums of gospel material in R&B settings. Over the past twenty years, the Winanses have attained international status as super-stars of gospel, R&B, and Christian worship music.

Yamatohime, Empress (c. 230–240) Yamatohime was an empress of Japan and also known as Queen Himiko of Yamatei. Her poem appears in *One Hundred Poems from the Japanese*, translated by Kenneth Rexroth.

Credits

The author is grateful to the following authors and publishers for permission to reproduce the material listed below. This page constitutes a continuation of the copyright page.

Victoria Lena Manyarrows for her poem from *Songs from the Native Lands* (San Francisco: Nopal Press, 1995).

Janice Mirikitani for her poem "Breaking Tradition" from *Breaking Silence: An Anthology of Contemporary Asian-American Poets*, edited by Joseph Bruchac (Greenfield Center, N.Y.: The Greenfield Review Press, 1983).

Toni Morrison for excerpts from *Beloved* (New York: Knopf, 1987) © 1987 by Toni Morrison, reprinted by permission of International Creative Management, Inc. and from *Paradise* (New York: Knopf, 1998).

Naomi Quinonez for her poem "My Shattered Sister" from *From Totems to Hip-Hop: A Multicultural Anthology of Poetry Across the Americas, 1900–2002*, edited by Ishmael Reed (New York: Thunder's Mouth Press, 2003).

Della Reese for excerpts from *What Is This Thing Called Love?* (Charlottesville, Va.: Hampton Roads Publishing) © 2001 by Rev. Della Reese.

Tawnicia Ferguson Rowan for contributing several of her unpublished poems.

Cathy Song for her poem "Lucky" from *Breaking Silence: An Anthology of Contemporary Asian-American Poets*, edited by Joseph Bruchac (Greenfield Center, N.Y.: The Greenfield Review Press, 1983).

Susan L. Taylor for excerpts from *Lessons in Living* (New York: Doubleday, 1995).

Acknowledgments

First and foremost, I'm so grateful to Dr. Monica A. Coleman, who is responsible for this project. Thanks for your confidence in me and your genuine friendship. To Omah Williams, thanks for your technical support (our secret). To Maura Shaw, the most patient woman walking on the face of the earth, you are the editor that every writer desperately needs. To Sarah McBride, for forcing me to remain focused and listening with an open spirit as this project reached the final stages. To Linda Roghaar, my literary agent, who made this process very easy for me. To my friends Danielle Charlton and Deniece Laster, thanks for your encouragement. With thanks to my Sunday school teachers, Mora Clarke, Rubelia Johnson, Frankie Johnson, and the late Aurelia Jackson, for teaching me the foundation of understanding who God is—LOVE. Many thanks to my father, Warren Jackson, and my brothers, Mark and Todd Jackson, for your support and protection, which has been invaluable. Last, but not least, I'm thankful to God for being my eternal source, strength, and hope.

Index of First Lines

Global Spiritual Perspectives

Spiritual Perspectives on America's Role as Superpower
by the Editors at SkyLight Paths

Are we the world's good neighbor or a global bully? Explores broader issues surrounding the use of American power around the world, including in Iraq and the Middle East. From a spiritual perspective, what are America's responsibilities as the only remaining superpower? Contributors:

Dr. Beatrice Bruteau • Rev. Dr. Joan Brown Campbell • Tony Campolo • Rev. Forrest Church • Lama Surya Das • Matthew Fox • Kabir Helminski • Thich Nhat Hanh • Eboo Patel • Abbot M. Basil Pennington, ocso • Dennis Prager • Rosemary Radford Ruether • Wayne Teasdale • Rev. William McD. Tully • Rabbi Arthur Waskow • John Wilson

5½ x 8½, 256 pp, Quality PB, ISBN 1-893361-81-0 **$16.95**

Spiritual Perspectives on Globalization, 2nd Edition
Making Sense of Economic and Cultural Upheaval
by Ira Rifkin; Foreword by Dr. David Little, Harvard Divinity School

What is globalization? What are spiritually minded people saying and doing about it? This lucid introduction surveys the religious landscape, explaining in clear and nonjudgmental language the beliefs that motivate spiritual leaders, activists, theologians, academics, and others involved on all sides of the issue. This edition includes a new Afterword and Discussion Guide designed for group use.

5½ x 8½, 256 pp, Quality PB, ISBN 1-59473-045-8 **$16.99**

Hinduism / Vedanta

Meditation & Its Practices: A Definitive Guide to Techniques and Traditions of Meditation in Yoga and Vedanta
by Swami Adiswarananda

The complete sourcebook for exploring Hinduism's two most time-honored traditions of meditation. Drawing on both classic and contemporary sources, this comprehensive sourcebook outlines the scientific, psychological, and spiritual elements of Yoga and Vedanta meditation.

6 x 9, 504 pp, HC, ISBN 1-893361-83-7 **$34.95**

Sri Sarada Devi: Her Teachings and Conversations
Translated and with Notes by Swami Nikhilananda
Edited and with an Introduction by Swami Adiswarananda

Brings to life the Holy Mother's teachings on human affliction, self-control, and peace in ways both personal and profound, and illuminates her role as the power, scripture, joy, and guiding spirit of the Ramakrishna Order.

6 x 9, 288 pp, HC, ISBN 1-59473-070-9 **$29.99**

The Vedanta Way to Peace and Happiness
by Swami Adiswarananda

Using language that is accessible to people of all faiths and backgrounds, this book introduces the timeless teachings of Vedanta—divinity of the individual soul, unity of all existence, and oneness with the Divine—ancient wisdom as relevant to human happiness today as it was thousands of years ago.

6 x 9, 240 pp, HC, ISBN 1-59473-034-2 **$29.99**

Spiritual Biography—SkyLight Lives

SkyLight Lives reintroduces the lives and works of key spiritual figures of our time—people who by their teaching or example have challenged our assumptions about spirituality and have caused us to look at it in new ways.

   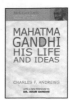

The Life of Evelyn Underhill
An Intimate Portrait of the Groundbreaking Author of *Mysticism*
by Margaret Cropper; Foreword by Dana Greene

Evelyn Underhill was a passionate writer and teacher who wrote elegantly on mysticism, worship, and devotional life. This is the story of how she made her way toward spiritual maturity, from her early days of agnosticism to the years when her influence was felt throughout the world.
6 x 9, 288 pp, 5 b/w photos, Quality PB, ISBN 1-893361-70-5 **$18.95**

Mahatma Gandhi: His Life and Ideas
by Charles F. Andrews; Foreword by Dr. Arun Gandhi

Examines from a contemporary Christian activist's point of view the religious ideas and political dynamics that influenced the birth of the peaceful resistance movement, the primary tool that Gandhi and the people of his homeland would use to gain India its freedom from British rule.
6 x 9, 336 pp, 5 b/w photos, Quality PB, ISBN 1-893361-89-6 **$18.95**

Simone Weil: A Modern Pilgrimage
by Robert Coles

The extraordinary life of the spiritual philosopher who's been called both saint and madwoman. Robert Coles' intriguing study of Weil is an insightful portrait of the beloved and controversial thinker whose life and writings influenced many (from T. S. Eliot to Adrienne Rich to Albert Camus), and continue to inspire seekers everywhere.
6 x 9, 208 pp, Quality PB, ISBN 1-893361-34-9 **$16.95**

Zen Effects: The Life of Alan Watts
by Monica Furlong

Through his widely popular books and lectures, Alan Watts (1915–1973) did more to introduce Eastern philosophy and religion to Western minds than any figure before or since. Here is the first and only full-length biography of one of the most charismatic spiritual leaders of the twentieth century.
6 x 9, 264 pp, Quality PB, ISBN 1-893361-32-2 **$16.95**

More Spiritual Biography

Bede Griffiths: An Introduction to His Interspiritual Thought
 by Wayne Teasdale 6 x 9, 288 pp, Quality PB, ISBN 1-893361-77-2 **$18.95**

Inspired Lives: Exploring the Role of Faith and Spirituality in the Lives of Extraordinary People
 by Joanna Laufer and Kenneth S. Lewis 6 x 9, 256 pp, Quality PB, ISBN 1-893361-33-0 **$16.95**

Spiritual Innovators: Seventy-Five Extraordinary People Who Changed the World in
 the Past Century   *Edited by Ira Rifkin and the Editors at SkyLight Paths; Foreword by Robert Coles*
 6 x 9, 304 pp, b/w photographs, Quality PB, ISBN 1-893361-50-0 **$16.95**; HC, ISBN 1-893361-43-8 **$24.95**

White Fire: A Portrait of Women Spiritual Leaders in America
 by Rabbi Malka Drucker; Photographs by Gay Block
 7 x 10, 320 pp, 30+ b/w photos, HC, ISBN 1-893361-64-0 **$24.95**

Spiritual Poetry—The Mystic Poets

Experience these mystic poets as you never have before. Each beautiful, compact book includes: A brief introduction to the poet's time and place; a summary of the major themes of the poet's mysticism and religious tradition; essential selections from the poet's most important works; and an appreciative preface by a contemporary spiritual writer.

 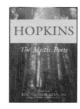  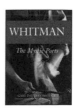

Hafiz: The Mystic Poets
Preface by Ibrahim Gamard
Hafiz is known throughout the world as Persia's greatest poet, with sales of his poems in Iran today only surpassed by those of the Qur'an itself. His probing and joyful verse speaks to people from all backgrounds who long to taste and feel divine love and experience harmony with all living things.
5 x 7¼, 144 pp, HC, ISBN 1-59473-009-1 **$16.99**

Hopkins: The Mystic Poets
Preface by Rev. Thomas Ryan, CSP
Gerard Manley Hopkins, Christian mystical poet, is beloved for his use of fresh language and startling metaphors to describe the world around him. Although his verse is lovely, beneath the surface lies a searching soul, wrestling with and yearning for God.
5 x 7¼, 112 pp, HC, ISBN 1-59473-010-5 **$16.99**

Tagore: The Mystic Poets
Preface by Swami Adiswarananda
Rabindranath Tagore is often considered the "Shakespeare" of modern India. A great mystic, Tagore was the teacher of W. B. Yeats and Robert Frost, the close friend of Albert Einstein and Mahatma Gandhi, and the winner of the Nobel Prize for Literature. This beautiful sampling of Tagore's two most important works, *The Gardener* and *Gitanjali,* offers a glimpse into his spiritual vision that has inspired people around the world.
5 x 7¼, 144 pp, HC, ISBN 1-59473-008-3 **$16.99**

Whitman: The Mystic Poets
Preface by Gary David Comstock
Walt Whitman was the most innovative and influential poet of the nineteenth century. This beautiful sampling of Whitman's most important poetry from *Leaves of Grass,* and selections from his prose writings, offers a glimpse into the spiritual side of his most radical themes—love for country, love for others, and love of Self.
5 x 7¼, 192 pp, HC, ISBN 1-59473-041-5 **$16.99**

Sacred Texts—SkyLight Illuminations Series
Andrew Harvey, series editor

Offers today's spiritual seeker an enjoyable entry into the great classic texts of the world's spiritual traditions. Each classic is presented in an accessible translation, with facing pages of guided commentary from experts, giving you the keys you need to understand the history, context, and meaning of the text. This series enables readers of all backgrounds to experience and understand classic spiritual texts directly, and to make them a part of their lives. Andrew Harvey writes the foreword to each volume, an insightful, personal introduction to each classic.

Bhagavad Gita
Annotated & Explained
Translation by Shri Purohit Swami; Annotation by Kendra Crossen Burroughs
"The very best Gita for first-time readers." —Ken Wilber. Millions of people turn daily to India's most beloved holy book, whose universal appeal has made it popular with non-Hindus and Hindus alike. This edition introduces you to the characters, explains references and philosophical terms, shares the interpretations of famous spiritual leaders and scholars, and more.
5½ x 8½, 192 pp, Quality PB, ISBN 1-893361-28-4 **$16.95**

Dhammapada
Annotated & Explained
Translation by Max Müller and revised by Jack Maguire; Annotation by Jack Maguire
The Dhammapada—believed to have been spoken by the Buddha himself over 2,500 years ago—contain most of Buddhism's central teachings. This timeless text concisely and inspirationally portrays the route a person travels as he or she advances toward enlightenment and describes the fundamental role of mental conditioning in making us who we are.
5½ x 8½, 160 pp, b/w photographs, Quality PB, ISBN 1-893361-42-X **$14.95**

The Gospel of Thomas
Annotated & Explained
Translation and annotation by Stevan Davies
Discovered in 1945, this collection of aphoristic sayings sheds new light on the origins of Christianity and the intriguing figure of Jesus, portraying the Kingdom of God as a present fact about the world, rather than a future promise or future threat.
5½ x 8½, 192 pp, Quality PB, ISBN 1-893361-45-4 **$16.95**

Hasidic Tales
Annotated & Explained
Translation and annotation by Rabbi Rami Shapiro
Introduces the legendary tales of the impassioned Hasidic rabbis, which demonstrate the spiritual power of unabashed joy, offer lessons for leading a holy life, and remind us that the Divine can be found in the everyday.
5½ x 8½, 240 pp, Quality PB, ISBN 1-893361-86-1 **$16.95**

The Hebrew Prophets
Selections Annotated & Explained
Translation and annotation by Rabbi Rami Shapiro
Focuses on the central themes covered by all the Hebrew prophets: moving from ignorance to wisdom, injustice to justice, cruelty to compassion, and despair to joy, and challenges us to engage in justice, kindness, and humility in every aspect of our lives.
5½ x 8½, 224 pp, Quality PB, ISBN 1-59473-037-7 **$16.99**

Sacred Texts—SkyLight Illuminations Series
Andrew Harvey, series editor

The Hidden Gospel of Matthew: Annotated & Explained
Translation and annotation by Ron Miller
Takes you deep into the text cherished around the world to discover the words and events that have the strongest connection to the historical Jesus. Reveals the underlying story of Matthew, a story that transcends the traditional theme of an atoning death and focuses instead on Jesus's radical call for personal transformation and social change.
5½ x 8½, 272 pp, Quality PB, ISBN 1-59473-038-5 **$16.99**

The Secret Book of John
The Gnostic Gospel—Annotated & Explained
Translation and annotation by Stevan Davies
Introduces the most significant and influential text of the ancient Gnostic religion. This central myth of Gnosticism tells the story of how God fell from perfect Oneness to imprisonment in the material world, and how by knowing our divine nature and our divine origins—that we are one with God—we reverse God's descent and find our salvation.
5½ x 8½, 208 pp, Quality PB, ISBN 1-59473-082-2 **$16.99**

Rumi and Islam: Selections from His Stories, Poems, and Discourses—Annotated & Explained
Translation and annotation by Ibrahim Gamard
Offers a new way of thinking about Rumi's poetry. Focuses on Rumi's place within the Sufi tradition of Islam, providing insight into the mystical side of the religion—one that has love of God at its core and sublime wisdom teachings as its pathways.
5½ x 8½, 240 pp, Quality PB, ISBN 1-59473-002-4 **$15.99**

Selections from the Gospel of Sri Ramakrishna
Annotated & Explained
Translation by Swami Nikhilananda; Annotation by Kendra Crossen Burroughs
The words of India's greatest example of God-consciousness and mystical ecstasy in recent history. Introduces the fascinating world of the Indian mystic and the universal appeal of his message that has inspired millions of devotees for more than a century.
5½ x 8½, 240 pp, b/w photographs, Quality PB, ISBN 1-893361-46-2 **$16.95**

The Way of a Pilgrim: Annotated & Explained
Translation and annotation by Gleb Pokrovsky
This classic of Russian spirituality is the delightful account of one man who sets out to learn the prayer of the heart—also known as the "Jesus prayer"—and how the practice transforms his life.
5½ x 8½, 160 pp, Illus., Quality PB, ISBN 1-893361-31-4 **$14.95**

Zohar: Annotated & Explained
Translation and annotation by Daniel C. Matt
The best-selling author of *The Essential Kabbalah* brings together in one place the most important teachings of the Zohar, the canonical text of Jewish mystical tradition. Guides you step by step through the midrash, mystical fantasy, and Hebrew scripture that make up the Zohar, explaining the inner meanings in facing-page commentary.
5½ x 8½, 176 pp, Quality PB, ISBN 1-893361-51-9 **$15.99**

Midrash Fiction

Daughters of the Desert: Tales of Remarkable Women from Christian, Jewish, and Muslim Traditions   *by Claire Rudolf Murphy, Meghan Nuttall Sayres, Mary Cronk Farrell, Sarah Conover, and Betsy Wharton*

Breathes new life into the old tales of our female ancestors in faith. Uses traditional scriptural passages as starting points, then with vivid detail fills in historical context and place. Chapters reveal the voices of Sarah, Hagar, Huldah, Esther, Salome, Mary Magdalene, Lydia, Khadija, Fatima, and many more. Historical fiction ideal for readers of all ages.

5½ x 8½, 192 pp, Quality PB, ISBN 1-59473-106-3 **$14.99**; HC, ISBN 1-893361-72-1 **$19.95**

The Triumph of Eve & Other Subversive Bible Tales
by Matt Biers-Ariel

Many people were taught and remember only a one-dimensional Bible. These engaging retellings are the antidote to this—they're witty, often hilarious, always profound, and invite you to grapple with questions and issues that are often hidden in the original text.

5½ x 8½, 192 pp, HC, ISBN 1-59473-040-7 **$19.99**

Religious Etiquette / Reference

How to Be a Perfect Stranger, 3rd Edition: The Essential Religious Etiquette Handbook   *Edited by Stuart M. Matlins and Arthur J. Magida*

The indispensable guidebook to help the well-meaning guest when visiting other people's religious ceremonies. A straightforward guide to the rituals and celebrations of the major religions and denominations in the United States and Canada from the perspective of an interested guest of any other faith, based on information obtained from authorities of each religion. Belongs in every living room, library, and office. Covers:

African American Methodist Churches • Assemblies of God • Baha'i • Baptist • Buddhist • Christian Church (Disciples of Christ) • Christian Science (Church of Christ, Scientist) • Churches of Christ • Episcopalian and Anglican • Hindu • Islam • Jehovah's Witnesses • Jewish • Lutheran • Mennonite/Amish • Methodist • Mormon (Church of Jesus Christ of Latter-day Saints) • Native American/First Nations • Orthodox Churches • Pentecostal Church of God • Presbyterian • Quaker (Religious Society of Friends) • Reformed Church in America/Canada • Roman Catholic • Seventh-day Adventist • Sikh • Unitarian Universalist • United Church of Canada • United Church of Christ

6 x 9, 432 pp, Quality PB, ISBN 1-893361-67-5 **$19.95**

The Perfect Stranger's Guide to Funerals and Grieving Practices: A Guide to Etiquette in Other People's Religious Ceremonies   *Edited by Stuart M. Matlins*

6 x 9, 240 pp, Quality PB, ISBN 1-893361-20-9 **$16.95**

The Perfect Stranger's Guide to Wedding Ceremonies: A Guide to Etiquette in Other People's Religious Ceremonies   *Edited by Stuart M. Matlins*

6 x 9, 208 pp, Quality PB, ISBN 1-893361-19-5 **$16.95**

Spirituality

Autumn: A Spiritual Biography of the Season
Edited by Gary Schmidt and Susan M. Felch; Illustrations by Mary Azarian
Autumn is a season of fruition and harvest, of thanksgiving and celebration of abundance and goodness of the earth. But it is also a season that starkly and realistically encourages us to see the limitations of our time. Warm and poignant pieces by Wendell Berry, David James Duncan, Robert Frost, A. Bartlett Giamatti, Kimiko Hahn, P. D. James, Julian of Norwich, Garret Keizer, Tracy Kidder, Anne Lamott, May Sarton, and many others rejoice in autumn as a time of preparation and reflection. 6 x 9, 320 pp, 5 b/w illus., HC, ISBN 1-59473-005-9 **$22.99**

Awakening the Spirit, Inspiring the Soul
30 Stories of Interspiritual Discovery in the Community of Faiths
Edited by Brother Wayne Teasdale and Martha Howard, MD; Foreword by Joan Borysenko, PhD
Thirty original spiritual mini-biographies that showcase the varied ways that people come to faith—and what that means—in today's multi-religious world.
6 x 9, 224 pp, HC, ISBN 1-59473-039-3 **$21.99**

Winter: A Spiritual Biography of the Season
Edited by Gary Schmidt and Susan M. Felch; Illustrations by Barry Moser
Delves into the varied feelings that winter conjures in us, calling up both the barrenness and the beauty of the natural world in wintertime. Includes selections by Will Campbell, Rachel Carson, Annie Dillard, Donald Hall, Ron Hansen, Jane Kenyon, Jamaica Kincaid, Barry Lopez, Kathleen Norris, John Updike, E. B. White, and many others. "This outstanding anthology features top-flight nature and spirituality writers on the fierce, inexorable season of winter.... Remarkably lively and warm, despite the icy subject." —*Publishers Weekly* Starred Review
6 x 9, 288 pp, 6 b/w illus., Deluxe PB w/flaps, ISBN 1-893361-92-6 **$18.95**; HC, ISBN 1-893361-53-5 **$21.95**

The Alphabet of Paradise: An A–Z of Spirituality for Everyday Life
by Howard Cooper 5 x 7¼, 224 pp, Quality PB, ISBN 1-893361-80-2 **$16.95**

Creating a Spiritual Retirement: A Guide to the Unseen Possibilities in Our Lives
by Molly Srode 6 x 9, 208 pp, b/w photos, Quality PB, ISBN 1-59473-050-42 **$14.99**;
HC, ISBN 1-893361-75-6 **$19.95**

The Geography of Faith: Underground Conversations on Religious, Political and Social Change *by Daniel Berrigan and Robert Coles; Updated introduction and afterword by the authors* 6 x 9, 224 pp, Quality PB, ISBN 1-893361-40-3 **$16.95**

God Lives in Glass: Reflections of God for Adults through the Eyes of Children
by Robert J. Landy, PhD; Foreword by Sandy Eisenberg Sasso
7 x 6, 64 pp, HC, Full-color illus., ISBN 1-893361-30-6 **$12.95**

God Within: Our Spiritual Future—As Told by Today's New Adults *Edited by Jon M. Sweeney and the Editors at SkyLight Paths* 6 x 9, 176 pp, Quality PB, ISBN 1-893361-15-2 **$14.95**

Jewish Spirituality: A Brief Introduction for Christians *by Lawrence Kushner*
5½ x 8½, 112 pp, Quality PB, ISBN 1-58023-150-0 **$12.95** *(a Jewish Lights book)*

A Jewish Understanding of the New Testament
by Rabbi Samuel Sandmel; New preface by Rabbi David Sandmel
5½ x 8½, 384 pp, Quality PB, ISBN 1-59473-048-2 **$19.99**

Journeys of Simplicity: Traveling Light with Thomas Merton, Basho, Edward Abbey, Annie Dillard & Others *by Philip Harnden* 5 x 7¼, 128 pp, HC, ISBN 1-893361-76-4 **$16.95**

Keeping Spiritual Balance As We Grow Older: More than 65 Creative Ways to Use Purpose, Prayer, and the Power of Spirit to Build a Meaningful Retirement
by Molly and Bernie Srode 8 x 8, 224 pp, Quality PB, ISBN 1-59473-042-3 **$16.99**

The Monks of Mount Athos: A Western Monk's Extraordinary Spiritual Journey on Eastern Holy Ground *by M. Basil Pennington, ocso; Foreword by Archimandrite Dionysios*
6 x 9, 256 pp, 10+ b/w line drawings, Quality PB, ISBN 1-893361-78-0 **$18.95**

One God Clapping: The Spiritual Path of a Zen Rabbi *by Alan Lew with Sherril Jaffe*
5½ x 8½, 336 pp, Quality PB, ISBN 1-58023-115-2 **$16.95** *(a Jewish Lights book)*

Spirituality

Prayer for People Who Think Too Much
A Guide to Everyday, Anywhere Prayer from the World's Faith Traditions   *by Mitch Finley*
5½ x 8½, 224 pp, Quality PB, ISBN 1-893361-21-7 **$16.95**; HC, ISBN 1-893361-00-4 **$21.95**

The Shaman's Quest: Journeys in an Ancient Spiritual Practice
by Nevill Drury; with a Basic Introduction to Shamanism by Tom Cowan
5½ x 8½, 208 pp, Quality PB, ISBN 1-893361-68-3 **$16.95**

Show Me Your Way: The Complete Guide to Exploring Interfaith Spiritual Direction
by Howard A. Addison   5½ x 8½, 240 pp, Quality PB, ISBN 1-893361-41-1 **$16.95**;
HC, ISBN 1-893361-12-8 **$21.95**

Spirituality 101: The Indispensable Guide to Keeping—or Finding—Your Spiritual Life
on Campus   *by Harriet L. Schwartz, with contributions from college students at nearly thirty campuses across the United States*   6 x 9, 272 pp, Quality PB, ISBN 1-59473-000-8 **$16.99**

Spiritually Incorrect: Finding God in All the Wrong Places
by Dan Wakefield; Illus. by Marian DelVecchio
5½ x 8½, 192 pp, b/w illus., HC, ISBN 1-893361-88-8 **$21.95**

Spiritual Manifestos: Visions for Renewed Religious Life in America from Young
Spiritual Leaders of Many Faiths   *Edited by Niles Elliot Goldstein; Preface by Martin E. Marty*
6 x 9, 256 pp, HC, ISBN 1-893361-09-8 **$21.95**

A Walk with Four Spiritual Guides: Krishna, Buddha, Jesus, and Ramakrishna
by Andrew Harvey 5½ x 8½, 192 pp, 10 b/w photos & illus., HC, ISBN 1-893361-73-X **$21.95**

What Matters: Spiritual Nourishment for Head and Heart
by Frederick Franck 5 x 7¼, 144 pp, 50+ b/w illus., HC, ISBN 1-59473-013-X **$16.99**

Who Is My God?, 2nd Edition
An Innovative Guide to Finding Your Spiritual Identity
Created by the Editors at SkyLight Paths 6 x 9, 160 pp, Quality PB, ISBN 1-59473-014-8 **$15.99**

Spirituality—A Week Inside

Come and Sit: A Week Inside Meditation Centers
by Marcia Z. Nelson; Foreword by Wayne Teasdale
The insider's guide to meditation in a variety of different spiritual traditions.
Traveling through Buddhist, Hindu, Christian, Jewish, and Sufi traditions, this essential guide takes you to different meditation centers to meet the teachers and students and learn about the practices, demystifying the meditation experience.
6 x 9, 224 pp, b/w photographs, Quality PB, ISBN 1-893361-35-7 **$16.95**

Lighting the Lamp of Wisdom: A Week Inside a Yoga Ashram
by John Ittner; Foreword by Dr. David Frawley
This insider's guide to Hindu spiritual life takes you into a typical week of retreat inside a yoga ashram to demystify the experience and show you what to expect from your own visit. Includes a discussion of worship services, meditation and yoga classes, chanting and music, work practice, and more.   6 x 9, 192 pp, b/w photographs, Quality PB, ISBN 1-893361-52-7 **$15.95**; HC, ISBN 1-893361-37-3 **$24.95**

Making a Heart for God: A Week Inside a Catholic Monastery
by Dianne Aprile; Foreword by Brother Patrick Hart, ocso
This essential guide to experiencing life in a Catholic monastery takes you to the Abbey of Gethsemani—the Trappist monastery in Kentucky that was home to author Thomas Merton—to explore the details. "More balanced and informative than the popular *The Cloister Walk* by Kathleen Norris." —*Choice: Current Reviews for Academic Libraries* 6 x 9, 224 pp, b/w photographs, Quality PB, ISBN 1-893361-49-7 **$16.95**; HC, ISBN 1-893361-14-4 **$21.95**

Waking Up: A Week Inside a Zen Monastery
by Jack Maguire; Foreword by John Daido Loori, Roshi
An essential guide to what it's like to spend a week inside a Zen Buddhist monastery.
6 x 9, 224 pp, b/w photographs, Quality PB, ISBN 1-893361-55-1 **$16.95**;
HC, ISBN 1-893361-13-6 **$21.95**

Children's Spirituality

God Said Amen
by Sandy Eisenberg Sasso; Full-color illus. by Avi Katz
A warm and inspiring tale of two kingdoms that shows us that we need
only reach out to each other to find the answers to our prayers.
9 x 12, 32 pp, HC, Full-color illus., ISBN 1 58023 080 6 **$16.95**
For ages 4 & up (a Jewish Lights book)

How Does God Listen?
by Kay Lindahl; Full-color photo illus. by Cynthia Maloney
How do we know when God is listening to us? Children will find the
answers to these questions as they engage their senses while the story
unfolds, learning how God listens in the wind, waves, clouds, hot choco-
late, perfume, our tears and our laughter.
10 x 8½, 32 pp, Quality PB, Full-color photo illus., ISBN 1-59473-084-9 **$8.99**
For ages 3–6

In God's Name
by Sandy Eisenberg Sasso; Full-color illus. by Phoebe Stone
Like an ancient myth in its poetic text and vibrant illustrations, this
award-winning modern fable about the search for God's name celebrates
the diversity and, at the same time, the unity of all the people of the world.
9 x 12, 32 pp, HC, Full-color illus., ISBN 1-879045-26-5 **$16.95**
For ages 4 & up (a Jewish Lights book)

Also available in Spanish:
El nombre de Dios
9 x 12, 32 pp, HC, Full-color illus., ISBN 1-893361-63-2 **$16.95**

Where Does God Live?
by August Gold; Full-color photo illus. by Matthew J. Perlman
Using simple, everyday examples that children can relate to, this colorful
book helps young readers develop a personal understanding of God.
10 x 8½, 32 pp, Quality PB, Full-color photo illus., ISBN 1-893361-39-X **$8.99**
For ages 3–6

In Our Image: God's First Creatures
by Nancy Sohn Swartz; Full-color illus. by Melanie Hall
A playful new twist on the Creation story—from the perspective of the
animals. Celebrates the interconnectedness of nature and the harmony of
all living things.   9 x 12, 32 pp, HC, Full-color illus., ISBN 1-879045-99-0 **$16.95**
For ages 4 & up (a Jewish Lights book)

Noah's Wife: The Story of Naamah
by Sandy Eisenberg Sasso; Full-color illus. by Bethanne Andersen
This new story, based on an ancient text, opens readers' religious imaginations
to new ideas about the well-known story of the Flood. When God tells Noah
to bring the animals of the world onto the ark, God also calls on Naamah,
Noah's wife, to save each plant on Earth.
9 x 12, 32 pp, HC, Full-color illus., ISBN 1-58023-134-9 **$16.95**
For ages 4 & up (a Jewish Lights book)

Also available:
Naamah: Noah's Wife (A Board Book)
by Sandy Eisenberg Sasso, Full-color illus by Bethanne Andersen
5 x 5, 24 pp, Board Book, Full-color illus., ISBN 1-893361-56-X **$7.99** *For ages 0–4*

Children's Spirituality—Board Books

How Did the Animals Help God? (A Board Book)
by Nancy Sohn Swartz, Full-color illus. by Melanie Hall
Abridged from Nancy Sohn Swartz's *In Our Image*, God asks all of nature to offer gifts to humankind—with a promise that they will care for creation in return.
5 x 5, 24 pp, Board Book, Full-color illus., ISBN 1-59473-044-X **$7.99** *For ages 0–4*

Where Is God? (A Board Book)
by Lawrence and Karen Kushner; Full-color illus. by Dawn W. Majewski
A gentle way for young children to explore how God is with us every day, in every way. Abridged from *Because Nothing Looks Like God* by Lawrence and Karen Kushner.   5 x 5, 24 pp, Board, Full-color illus., ISBN 1-893361-17-9 **$7.95** *For ages 0–4*

What Does God Look Like? (A Board Book)
by Lawrence and Karen Kushner; Full-color illus. by Dawn W. Majewski
A simple way for young children to explore the ways that we "see" God. Abridged from *Because Nothing Looks Like God* by Lawrence and Karen Kushner.
5 x 5, 24 pp, Board, Full-color illus., ISBN 1-893361-23-3 **$7.95** *For ages 0–4*

How Does God Make Things Happen? (A Board Book)
by Lawrence and Karen Kushner; Full-color illus. by Dawn W. Majewski
A charming invitation for young children to explore how God makes things happen in our world. Abridged from *Because Nothing Looks Like God* by Lawrence and Karen Kushner.   5 x 5, 24 pp, Board, Full-color illus., ISBN 1-893361-24-1 **$7.95** *For ages 0–4*

What Is God's Name? (A Board Book)
by Sandy Eisenberg Sasso; Full-color illus. by Phoebe Stone
Everyone and everything in the world has a name. What is God's name? Abridged from the award-winning *In God's Name* by Sandy Eisenberg Sasso.
5 x 5, 24 pp, Board, Full-color illus., ISBN 1-893361-10-1 **$7.99** *For ages 0–4*

What You Will See Inside ...

This important new series of books is designed to show children ages 6–10 the Who, What, When, Where, Why and How of traditional houses of worship, liturgical celebrations, and rituals of different world faiths, empowering them to respect and understand their own religious traditions—and those of their friends and neighbors.

What You Will See Inside a Catholic Church
by Reverend Michael Keane; Foreword by Robert J. Keeley, Ed.D.
Full-color photographs by Aaron Pepis
A colorful, fun-to-read introduction to the traditions of Catholic worship and faith. Visually explores the common use of the altar, processional cross, baptismal font, votive candles, and more.   8½ x 10½, 32 pp, HC, ISBN 1-893361-54-3 **$17.95**

Also available in Spanish: **Lo que se puede ver dentro de una iglesia católica**
8½ x 10½, 32 pp, Full-color photos, HC, ISBN 1-893361-66-7 **$16.95**

What You Will See Inside a Mosque
by Aisha Karen Khan; Photographs by Aaron Pepis
Featuring full-page pictures and concise descriptions of what is happening, the objects used, the spiritual leaders and laypeople who have specific roles, and the spiritual intent of the believers. Demystifies the celebrations and ceremonies of Islam throughout the year.
8½ x 10½, 32 pp, Full-color photos, HC, ISBN 1-893361-60-8 **$16.95**

What You Will See Inside a Synagogue
by Rabbi Lawrence A. Hoffman and Dr. Ron Wolfson; Full-color photos by Bill Aron
A colorful, fun-to-read introduction that explains the ways and whys of Jewish worship and religious life. Full-page photos; concise but informative descriptions of the objects used, the clergy and laypeople who have specific roles, and much more.
8½ x 10½, 32 pp, Full-color photos, HC, ISBN 1-59473-012-1 **$17.99**

Children's Spiritual Biography

MULTICULTURAL, NONDENOMINATIONAL, NONSECTARIAN

Ten Amazing People
And How They Changed the World
by Maura D. Shaw; Foreword by Dr. Robert Coles
Full-color illus. by Stephen Marchesi

For ages 7 & up

Black Elk • Dorothy Day • Malcolm X • Mahatma Gandhi • Martin Luther King, Jr. • Mother Teresa • Janusz Korczak • Desmond Tutu • Thich Nhat Hanh • Albert Schweitzer

This vivid, inspirational, and authoritative book will open new possibilities for children by telling the stories of how ten of the past century's greatest leaders changed the world in important ways.

8½ x 11, 48 pp, HC, Full-color illus., ISBN 1-893361-47-0 **$17.95** *For ages 7 & up*

Spiritual Biographies for Young People—For ages 7 and up

Black Elk: Native American Man of Spirit
by Maura D. Shaw; Full-color illus. by Stephen Marchesi
Through historically accurate illustrations and photos, inspiring age-appropriate activities, and Black Elk's own words, this colorful biography introduces children to a remarkable person who ensured that the traditions and beliefs of his people would not be forgotten.
6¼ x 8¼, 32 pp, HC, Full-color illus., ISBN 1-59473-043-1 **$12.99**

Dorothy Day: A Catholic Life of Action
by Maura D. Shaw; Full-color illus. by Stephen Marchesi
Introduces children to one of the most inspiring women of the twentieth century, a down-to-earth spiritual leader who saw the presence of God in every person she met. Includes practical activities, a timeline, and a list of important words to know.
6¼ x 8¼, 32 pp, HC, Full-color illus., ISBN 1-59473-011-3 **$12.99**

Gandhi: India's Great Soul
by Maura D. Shaw; Full-color illus. by Stephen Marchesi
There are a number of biographies of Gandhi written for young readers, but this is the only one that balances a simple text with illustrations, photographs, and activities that encourage children and adults to talk about how to make changes happen without violence. Introduces children to important concepts of freedom, equality, and justice among people of all backgrounds and religions.
6¼ x 8¼, 32 pp, HC, Full-color illus., ISBN 1-893361-91-8 **$12.95**

Thich Nhat Hanh: Buddhism in Action
by Maura D. Shaw; Full-color illus. by Stephen Marchesi
Warm illustrations, photos, age-appropriate activities, and Thich Nhat Hanh's own poems introduce a great man to children in a way they can understand and enjoy. Includes a list of important Buddhist words to know.
6¼ x 8¼, 32 pp, HC, Full-color illus., ISBN 1-893361-87-X **$12.95**

Kabbalah *from Jewish Lights Publishing*

Ehyeh: A Kabbalah for Tomorrow *by Dr. Arthur Green*
6 x 9, 224 pp, Quality PB, ISBN 1-58023-213-2 **$16.99;** HC, ISBN 1-58023-125-X **$21.95**

The Enneagram and Kabbalah: Reading Your Soul *by Rabbi Howard A. Addison*
6 x 9, 176 pp, Quality PB, ISBN 1-58023-001-6 **$15.95**

Finding Joy: A Practical Spiritual Guide to Happiness *by Dannel I. Schwartz with Mark Hass*
6 x 9, 192 pp, Quality PB, ISBN 1-58023-009-1 **$14.95;** HC, ISBN 1-879045-53-2 **$19.95**

The Gift of Kabbalah: Discovering the Secrets of Heaven, Renewing Your Life on Earth
by Tamar Frankiel, Ph.D.
6 x 9, 256 pp, Quality PB, ISBN 1-58023-141-1 **$16.95;** HC, ISBN 1-58023-108-X **$21.95**

Zohar: Annotated & Explained
Translation and annotation by Dr. Daniel C. Matt. Foreword by Andrew Harvey
5½ x 8½, 160 pp, Quality PB, ISBN 1-893361-51-9 **$15.99**

Meditation / Prayer

Prayers to an Evolutionary God
by William Cleary; Afterword by Diarmuid O'Murchu

How is it possible to pray when God is dislocated from heaven, dispersed all around us, and more of a creative force than an all-knowing father? Inspired by the spiritual and scientific teachings of Diarmuid O'Murchu and Teilhard de Chardin, Cleary reveals that religion and science can be combined to create an expanding view of the universe—an evolutionary faith.
6 x 9, 208 pp, HC, ISBN 1-59473-006-7 **$21.99**

The Song of Songs: A Spiritual Commentary
by M. Basil Pennington, OCSO; Illustrations by Phillip Ratner

Join M. Basil Pennington as he ruminates on the Bible's most challenging mystical text. You will follow a path into the Songs that weaves through his inspired words and the evocative drawings of Jewish artist Phillip Ratner—a path that reveals your own humanity and leads to the deepest delight of your soul.
6 x 9, 160 pp, HC, 14 b/w illus., ISBN 1-59473-004-0 **$19.99**

Women of Color Pray: Voices of Strength, Faith, Healing,
Hope, and Courage   *Edited and with Introductions by Christal M. Jackson*

Through these prayers, poetry, lyrics, meditations and affirmations, you will share in the strong and undeniable connection women of color share with God. It will challenge you to explore new ways of prayerful expression.
5 x 7¼, 208 pp, Quality PB, ISBN 1-59473-077-6 **$15.99**

The Art of Public Prayer, 2nd Edition: Not for Clergy Only
by Lawrence A. Hoffman   6 x 9, 288 pp, Quality PB, ISBN 1-893361-06-3 **$18.95**

Finding Grace at the Center: The Beginning of Centering Prayer
by M. Basil Pennington, ocso, Thomas Keating, ocso, and Thomas E. Clarke, SJ
5 x 7¼, 112 pp, HC, ISBN 1-893361-69-1 **$14.95**

A Heart of Stillness: A Complete Guide to Learning the Art of Meditation
by David A. Cooper   5½ x 8½, 272 pp, Quality PB, ISBN 1-893361-03-9 **$16.95**

Meditation without Gurus: A Guide to the Heart of Practice
by Clark Strand   5½ x 8½, 192 pp, Quality PB, ISBN 1-893361-93-4 **$16.95**

Praying with Our Hands: Twenty-One Practices of Embodied Prayer from the
World's Spiritual Traditions   *by Jon M. Sweeney; Photographs by Jennifer J. Wilson; Foreword by Mother Tessa Bielecki; Afterword by Taitetsu Unno, PhD*
8 x 8, 96 pp, 22 duotone photographs, Quality PB, ISBN 1-893361-16-0 **$16.95**

Silence, Simplicity & Solitude: A Complete Guide to Spiritual Retreat at Home
by David A. Cooper   5½ x 8½, 336 pp, Quality PB, ISBN 1-893361-04-7 **$16.95**

Three Gates to Meditation Practice: A Personal Journey into Sufism, Buddhism, and Judaism   *by David A. Cooper*   5½ x 8½, 240 pp, Quality PB, ISBN 1-893361-22-5 **$16.95**

Women Pray: Voices through the Ages, from Many Faiths, Cultures, and Traditions
Edited and with introductions by Monica Furlong
5 x 7¼, 256 pp, Quality PB, ISBN 1-59473-071-7 **$15.99;**
Deluxe HC with ribbon marker, ISBN 1-893361-25-X **$19.95**